T0163504

TEXAS NATURAL HISTORY GUIDES™

VENOMOUS
SNAKES OF TEXAS

A FIELD GUIDE

ANDREW H. PRICE

UNIVERSITY OF TEXAS PRESS
Austin

Requests for permission to reproduce material from this work should be sent to:

> Permissions
> University of Texas Press
> P.O. Box 7819
> Austin, TX 78713-7819
> www.utexas.edu/utpress/about/bpermission.html

♾ The paper used in this book meets the minimum requirements of ANSI/NISO
Z39.48-1992 (R1997) (Permanence of Paper).

LIBRARY OF CONGRESS CATALOGING-IN-PUBLICATION DATA

This is a revised and updated edition of *Poisonous Snakes of Texas*, published in 1998
by Texas Parks and Wildlife Press.

Price, Andrew H. (Andrew Hoyt), 1951–
    Venomous snakes of Texas : a field guide / Andrew H. Price.
        p.   cm. — (Texas natural history guides)
    Rev. ed. of: Poisonous snakes of Texas.
    Includes bibliographical references and index.
    ISBN 978-0-292-71967-5 (pbk. : alk. paper)
    1. Poisonous snakes—Texas—Identification.   I. Price, Andrew H.
(Andrew Hoyt), 1951– Poisonous snakes of Texas.   II. Title.
    QL666.O6P74   2009
    597.96'16509764—dc22

                                                        2008049359

To all those
Texas herpetologists
who have befriended me
over the years
and given freely
of their time,
resources, and knowledge
about the herpetofauna
of this state.
I look forward
to our mutual enjoyment
of these wonderful animals
during my time left.

CONTENTS

PREFACE

This publication has been issued in a series of editions since 1950 by the Texas Parks and Wildlife Department in response to many requests for a condensed illustrated guide to the venomous snakes of Texas. Written initially to counter the widespread fear and misinformation regarding snakes and snakebite in Texas, the book has been expanded to further that mission. There is no doubt that a venomous snakebite can be a major medical emergency, and this book still serves the primary purpose of introducing the very latest knowledge concerning prevention and treatment. However, the text also introduces the reader to the ecological and evolutionary context in which these snakes live. I want to educate the interested reader about the myths and realities concerning the biological characteristics of Texas's venomous snakes. My desire is to lessen the hatred and fear and to increase the understanding, the respect, and even the appreciation with which venomous snakes should be regarded.

Fifteen kinds (species and subspecies) of venomous snakes are found in Texas. Each kind is illustrated herein by color photographs and range maps. Accompanying text provides the common and scientific name, a general description, a comparison with similar species found in Texas, and summary sketches of habitat, behavior, reproduction, predators and prey, venom, and fossil history. Terms that may be unfamiliar to the layperson are defined in the glossary. With this information, the reader should have little difficulty learning to recognize the venomous snakes found in specific parts of the state.

The references listed in the bibliography have been used in the preparation of this revised publication. In addition, I recommend the following sources to those who wish to delve deeper into the biology of venomous snakes in particular or the science of herpetology in general. One may wish to join a local herpetology club (there are many), a regional group (the Texas Herpetological Society, East Texas Herpetological Society, Dallas–Fort Worth Herpetological Society, West Texas Herpetological Society to name a few), or one of the three international U.S.-based societies devoted to the study of amphibians and reptiles. They are the American Society of Ichthyologists and Herpetologists (ASIH, founded in 1913, publisher of the journal *Copeia*), the Herpetologists' League (HL, founded in 1936, publisher of the journals *Herpetologica* and *Herpetological Monographs*), and the Society for the Study of Amphibians and Reptiles (SSAR, founded in 1967, publisher of the *Journal of Herpetology*, *Herpetological Review*, and *Catalogue of American Amphibians and Reptiles*, as well as a number of books and pamphlets). Interested readers may refer to their websites or call or write me for further information.

The line drawings in this book are from the 1998 edition. I am indebted to John E. Werler, the author of the 1950–1978 editions of this book, for his many years devoted to educating the people of Texas about their natural heritage. I appreciate the folks at the University of Texas Press, especially Bill Bishel and Victoria Davis, for suggesting the current revision in the first place, their patience with me, and their untiring editorial efforts to improve the outcome. I thank Janice F. Jackson of the Statistical Services

Division, Bureau of Vital Statistics, Texas Department of Health, for providing me with the updated figures on selected sources of mortality in Texas. I thank Drs. Jonathan A. Campbell (University of Texas at Arlington), Don Connell, MD (Austin, Texas), Richard C. Dart, MD (Rocky Mountain Poison and Drug Center, Denver, Colorado), James R. Dixon (Texas A&M University, emeritus), Frederick R. Gehlbach (Baylor University), Harry W. Greene (Cornell University), David L. Hardy, MD (Tucson, Arizona), Jerry D. Johnson (University of Texas at El Paso), William W. Lamar (Tyler, Texas), and Sherman A. Minton, MD (Indianapolis, Indiana, now deceased) for reviewing the 1998 version of this work; I am solely responsible for any errors of omission or commission in the current version. And finally I am profoundly grateful to my friends Mike Price, Craig Rudolf, and Tom Sinclair for allowing me to use their superb photographs, which have improved the quality of this book immeasurably.

VENOMOUS
SNAKES OF TEXAS

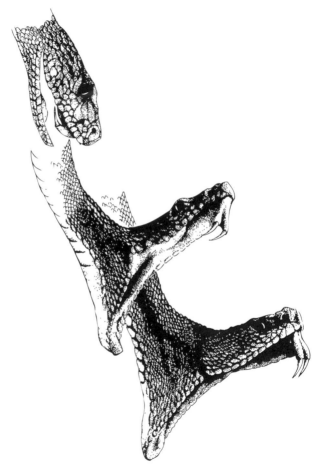

Sequence of a typical pit-viper strike: first, the fangs are folded up against the roof of the almost closed mouth; then the fangs become erect, pointing to the front of the mouth as it opens wide; the strike concludes with a bite.

INTRODUCTION

Although it is clear from the biological evidence that snakes and lizards are closely related, as reflected in the placement of the two groups within the same taxonomic category (the reptilian order Squamata), the precise origin of snakes remains uncertain. Snakes and lizards could have evolved as separate lineages from within an ancient group called the Lepidosauria, or they could have evolved from a common lepidosaurian ancestor. The most likely scenario is that snakes evolved from lizards, the earliest representatives of which appear in the fossil record some 230 million years ago, during the Paleozoic-Mesozoic transition. The earliest unambiguous snake fossil dates from the early Cretaceous, about 135 million years ago. Diversification of the snake clade (the group that includes all descendants of a common snake ancestor) occurred by the late Cretaceous-Paleocene transition (70–65 million years ago), and by the Miocene (22.5 million years ago) the dominant modern families (Colubridae, Elapidae, and

Viperidae) were present. Most biologists believe that ancestral snakes were adapted to a secretive or semiburrowing existence, as reflected by their descendants' possession of characteristics such as body elongation; modification of internal organs, including extreme elongation or loss of paired structure; loss of limbs; extreme reduction or loss of supporting pectoral and pelvic girdles; replacement of movable eyelids with a transparent cap over the eye; rearrangement and increased complexity of jaw and head muscles; and complete separation of mandibular symphyses, allowing each half of the lower jaw to be moved independently. There is some recent fossil evidence suggesting that the lizard ancestors of snakes may have been aquatic, seagoing forms, probably related to the mosasaurs—a group of giant marine lizards that became extinct at the same time as the dinosaurs. Many of the features listed above could just as readily be explained as aquatic adaptations. Whatever snakes' original line of descent, their ability to capture prey through constriction or the use of venom were later developments. Today, snakes, along with lizards, are the dominant reptiles on earth, and can be found on all continents except Antarctica and inhabit many oceans.

In today's society, where information about almost any subject is readily available, knowledge about venomous snakes and snakebite remains a relative mystery to most people. More than one recent survey has revealed that snakes in general possess a higher "fear quotient" for respondents than almost any other group of organisms, which probably reflects a relationship extending well into human prehistory. Given the abundance and diversity of snakes in Texas, and the increasing frequency with which Texans and visitors are exploring the outdoors, it is essential that accurate knowledge be available about the identification, distribution, and biological characteristics of the state's venomous reptiles, the relative risks of snakebite, and how to prevent it or treat it should it occur.

The first major study of the incidence of venomous snakebite in Texas was reported in 1927 by Afranio do Amaral, then director of the Antivenom Institute of America. During the twelve-month period from July 1926 to June 1927, a total of 150 cases of snakebite envenomation were known to have occurred in Texas, 28 of them fatal. A subsequent survey by R. H. Hutchison showed that 163 cases of snakebite were reported in 1928, 9 of which resulted in death. John Werler of the Houston Zoo recorded 1,318 snakebites in Texas during the five-year period 1949–1953, 18 of them fatal.

Henry M. Parrish reported on 559 snakebite cases seen by Texas physicians in 1958–1959. Of those, 461 were detailed enough to extract information. Rattlesnakes were involved in 47% of the cases, followed by copperheads (22%), cottonmouths (7%), coral snakes (1%), and a high number of unidentified venomous snakes (23%). Bites were less frequent in the sparsely populated western third of the state, and particularly high around larger cities (Austin, Beaumont, El Paso, Dallas/Fort Worth, Houston, Port Arthur, and San Antonio). Ninety-seven percent of all snakebites reported in the survey occurred during the months of April through November, when snakes are most active and when people are more likely to be outdoors. The largest number of bite victims (46%) were under 20 years of age, highlighting the importance both of supervising young children closely when they are in areas where venomous snakes are known to occur, and of instructing older children and teenagers in matters of snakebite prevention.

Most recently, T. G. Glass reported on 175 snakebite cases he personally treated in the San Antonio area from 1966 to 1975. The victims ranged in age from eighteen months to eighty-five years, with males being bitten more than twice as often as females (121 versus 54). The snakes inflicting the bites were western diamondback rattlesnakes (*Crotalus atrox*; 135, or 77%), copperheads (*Agkistrodon contortrix*; 30, or 17%), cottonmouths (*Agkistrodon piscivorus*; 5, or 3%), and coral snakes (*Micrurus fulvius*; 5, or 3%). Of those, 101 (75%) western diamondback, 19 (63%) copperhead, and 3 (60%) cottonmouth bites were treated surgically based on the appearance of local symptoms such as swelling or tenderness. This level of surgical intervention is considered unnecessary by most medical personnel today. Debridement (surgical removal of damaged tissue) revealed obvious signs of intramuscular injection of venom in 69 (56%) cases. Bites occurred most often on the leg (33%), followed by foot or ankle (28%), finger (20%), and hand or arm (15%). Fourteen patients developed blood-clotting problems, 16 were treated with antivenom, 13 developed serum sickness, and one eighty-five-year-old woman died from complete defibrination of the plasma resulting in a cerebral hemorrhage.

In general surveys of more than 1,300 snakebite cases from southern states during the 1960s and 1970s by L. H. S. Van Mierop and Henry Parrish and colleagues, 25% of the cases were "dry bites"—fang marks were present, but there was little if any pain because little or no venom was injected—and no medical treatment was necessary. Mild envenomation with slight swelling and pain occurred in 39% of the cases, requiring minimal medical treatment and usually no administration of antivenom. Moderate envenomation accompanied by pain, swelling, nausea, and other symptoms of shock occurred in 22%, requiring medical attention and the administration of antivenom. Finally, severe envenomation with heightened symptoms, including unconsciousness in some cases, occurred in 14%, requiring hospitalization and treatment with high levels of antivenom.

Snakebites are relatively rare when compared to accidents resulting from other outdoor-related activities, as shown by data from the Bureau of Vital Statistics, Texas Department of Health, in the table below.

One aim of the 1998 edition of this book was to reduce the incidence of snakebite by educating people about the nature of venomous snakes and by showing them how to be better prepared to deal with such a contingency during outdoor activities. Statistics show that the subsequent reduction in the rate of death from snakebite in Texas—especially when compared to increases in death rates from automobile accidents, boating accidents, and firearm accidents—may be attributed to the success of such educational efforts as well as to advances in medical treatment. I again urge every Texan to obtain a thorough working knowledge of the correct first-aid treatment for snakebite so that proper action may be taken if it becomes necessary. Preventing a bite from happening is at least equally important, and a necessary step toward attaining this goal is to acquire knowledge about the habits, distribution, behavior, and identification of

TABLE 1. Annual human deaths from selected outdoor activities in Texas, 1997–2005

YEAR	AUTO	DROWNING	NONDROWNING, BOATING	FIREARM, HUNTING	LIGHTNING	VENOMOUS ARTHROPOD	SNAKEBITE
1997	3,743	362	81	78	6	9	0
1998	3,748	391	57	74	5	2	0
1999	3,055	312	44	66	6	3	1
2000	3,807	326	59	58	4	5	1
2001	3,922	279	52	59	4	6	1
2002	3,979	295	55	52	6	13	0
2003	3,970	311	43	100	5	12	0
2004	3,808	270	45	104	4	13	0
2005	3,704	308	25	79	5	16	2

venomous snakes. A further step is to understand the evolutionary adaptations of venomous snakes and their ways and, in a larger sense, to reintegrate humankind with the natural world. This book is intended to be a small contribution toward that goal.

PRECAUTIONS AT HOME

Statistics show that a large percentage of all bites occur near the home. Although a few of these are inflicted upon small children playing in their own backyards, many are what physicians refer to as "illegitimate bites," resulting from people taking unnecessary or foolish risks with venomous snakes. Every year, zoos, animal control officers, and other wildlife-agency personnel receive calls from distressed homeowners who have discovered rattlesnakes or copperheads beneath their houses, in garages, or under trash piles. They ask for assistance in removing the snakes and preventing them from coming back. Unfortunately, as human populations grow, cities expand into snake habitats, and since greater numbers of people want to live near "natural" or "pristine" areas, such incidents will become only more frequent. Venomous snakes are a fact of life in Texas; encounters can be managed and minimized but not eliminated. Unfortunately, none of the commercially available "snake-proofing" devices, chemical or mechanical, have ever been demonstrated to be completely reliable.

Snakes, including the venomous kinds, frequent human areas for two basic reasons: food and shelter. Snakes are found in or underneath objects either because those objects also attract their prey, such as rodents, or because the snakes are escaping inhospitable weather conditions. One can therefore minimize the attractiveness of a dwelling to a venomous snake by moving the objects which attract rodents and other prey items, such as trash dumps, brush piles, and wood piles, and by constructing barns and livestock sheds as far away from dwellings as possible. Overturned boats, trailers, tarps, and similar objects may provide temporary shelter for a snake moving through the area. Snakes are adept at getting through seemingly impossibly tiny openings, which should be kept in mind when attempting to close off a basement, a detached garage, or a shed. Keep such areas as neat and tidy as possible, and remember that snakes seek out such areas for peace and quiet, and so are likely to be tucked away somewhere instead of lying in the middle of the floor.

Charles M. Bogert, late curator of herpetology at the American Museum of Natural History, once suggested the use of a quarter-inch mesh wire fencing to keep snakes off residential property. A yard-high, snakeproof fence would be placed around the house much like an ordinary picket fence, except that the bottom must be set about six inches down into the ground to prevent snakes from forcing their way beneath it. In addition, all gates must be provided with close-fitting sills on the bottoms and sides to ensure a completely tight enclosure. Experiments with fences of this kind were made to determine their effectiveness and to seek possible improvements in their construction, with the result that one important change was made. Copperheads and small rattlesnakes could not get over the vertically straight fence, but a six-foot rattlesnake used in the experiment was able to climb over. When the same fence was tilted outward at a 30-degree angle, not even the largest snake was able to reach the top. Although such fences are expensive and difficult to keep in good repair, they may be desirable under extreme circumstances.

Electrified fences have been tried in certain situations, such as the invasion of the Pacific island of Guam by the brown tree snake (*Boiga irregularis*), with some success. These fences are at least 2 feet (60 cm) high, and all vegetation is cleared away an equal distance from both sides of them. They are usually constructed of vinyl netting or similar material, and are most effective if several electrical strands are embedded in it.

PROTECTION IN THE FIELD

In rural areas, where venomous snakes are more common, they present a greater hazard to human life than elsewhere. Consequently, farmers, ranchers, hunters, fishermen, hikers, campers, and others who spend a great deal of time outdoors should take extra care in avoiding a bite. Because most snakebites are inflicted on the arms or legs, they require special protection. The use of a little caution when placing hands and feet where snakes may be partially or completely hidden from view is the best protection. This is particularly true when climbing on rocky ledges, where one's hands may reach a ledge before the eyes do. In some parts of the state, rattlesnakes and copperheads are common on rocky hillsides, where, especially during the warm days of early spring or late fall, they coil and sun themselves.

Pack rat middens and armadillo burrows also make excellent shelters for rattlesnakes, and it is foolhardy to reach into one of these holes. Yet, during one year in South Texas alone, two people were bitten by rattlesnakes when they reached into armadillo holes searching for small game animals.

Another way to invite snakebite is to turn over a log or similar object thoughtlessly with bare hands or to step over one without first looking to see if a snake is coiled on the other side. Many snakes, particularly copperheads and coral snakes, often hide beneath or within decaying logs, and such habitats should be considered a potential snake haven. If a log must be moved, use a long stick or garden tool. Stepping over a log will be less risky if boots or high-top shoes are worn, but even then it is safer to first see what is on the other side.

Several types of footwear offer good protection against the bites of most snakes, especially high-top leather shoes, riding boots, rubber boots, or a combination of army "paratrooper shoes" and heavy leather puttees. For protection of the legs above the knees, snakeproof trousers are available that weigh little more

Fig.1. Timber rattlesnake in ambush.
Photo by Craig Rudolf

than those of ordinary duck. They consist of three thicknesses of duck material and one layer of fine wire mesh, flexible enough to allow easy knee movement. Snakeproof leggings made of a similar material can be purchased for safeguarding just the lower legs. Aluminum or plastic leggings furnish good protection in many cases, but some brands may be thin and easily damaged, while others are simply uncomfortable.

If an active venomous snake is discovered nearby, the best response is to remain as still as possible until the snake has moved away. It should be remembered that a snake might be quick to strike at a moving object, so to step away at such a moment may stimulate the snake to strike. If a rattlesnake is heard nearby but cannot be located, do not make a wild dash for safety. The location of the snake may be misjudged, and a person fleeing the area may walk into rather than away from it. Again, remain still until the snake is sighted. When it is certain the reptile is at least five or six feet distant and is the only snake in the vicinity, slowly back away. If you must move away before locating the snake, do it as slowly as possible.

Because native venomous snakes are mostly nocturnal in their activities, usually remaining hidden during the day and emerging at night to search for food, a flashlight should be used by persons who find it necessary to travel on foot through snake country after dark. This precaution should be taken even around one's own home, particularly for those living in newly expanding suburbs or in rural areas. During the cooler days of spring and autumn, however, these daily habits are often reversed: snakes will be out during the day, searching for warm spots in which to sun themselves, and by nightfall they will again be under cover.

None of the types of venomous snakes found in Texas ordinarily can strike farther than a distance equal to three-quarters of its body length unless it has a firm backing or is striking downward on an incline. Certainly, none has the ability to jump at a target, a feat often attributed to rattlesnakes. A snake on the defensive is coiled, with the forward part of the body in a loose S position. When a snake strikes, this coil is straightened out and the head is thrust forward. It is not necessary for a snake to strike from a coil in order to bite; if picked up, it may simply turn and bite the hand that is holding it.

RECOGNIZING THE VENOMOUS KINDS OF SNAKES

The ability to differentiate harmless from venomous snakes is an important component of managing the risk and treatment of snakebite. Only 15 of the approximately 120 different kinds of snakes native to Texas are dangerous to humans, and some of these are so infrequently encountered that they are not much of a threat. In addition to these, several species of smaller Texas snakes known as opisthoglyphs ("rear-fanged") possess a relatively mild venom and a set of small, grooved fangs set far back on the upper jaw. They are considered harmless to humans because of their unaggressive behavior, weak and limited supply of venom, and small fangs, which are poorly adapted for injecting venom into large animals. Most of these, such as the black-headed snakes (genus *Tantilla*), which are found throughout the state, are less than 15 inches (38 cm) long and thinner than a pencil. The slightly larger night snake (*Hypsiglena torquata*) of west and central Texas has enlarged but ungrooved teeth in the upper jaw. Two Mexican species found as far north as the King Ranch (Norias Division) are somewhat larger: the black-striped snake (*Coniophanes imperialis*) reaches about 20 inches (50 cm), and the cat-eyed snake (*Leptodeira septentrionalis*) reaches about 36 inches (90 cm). Another rarely seen (but not rare) species is the lyre snake (*Trimorphodon biscutatus*) from extreme west Texas.

No single, general rule can be used to safely identify venomous snakes in Texas at a glance. For example, it is a mistaken idea that all venomous snakes have broad triangular heads. In fact, anyone applying this rule could mistake many of our harmless snakes for venomous ones. Hognose snakes (genus *Heterodon*), water snakes (genus *Nerodia*), and garter snakes (genus *Thamnophis*) can all flatten their heads by laterally expanding their jaw muscles as part of their defensive display, whereas the coral snake has a small, narrow head. The characteristic rattle of a rattlesnake may be missing under some circumstances, rendering identification more difficult. A rattlesnake may be coiled so that the rattle is hidden beneath the snake's body, and therefore the snake must be recognized by different means. Rattlesnakes frequently do not rattle before initially striking, so don't expect a warning—it might not come.

Disregard all of the so-called easy rules by which venomous snakes can be identified, and instead learn to know each one by the combination of its most characteristic features. For example, to identify the cottonmouth, look for a relatively short, stout body and a broad, flat head. Ignore the light color of the inside of the mouth. Also, look for a body color of black, dark brown, or olive and a pattern of ten to fifteen wide, usually indistinct crossbands that are generally lighter in the center than on the edges. The upper jaw below the eye and the lower jaw will be light colored, in contrast to the dark color of the remainder of the head. Together, these characteristics will make identification quite certain at a reasonable distance. Remember that the young of this species are colored differently from the adults and that you may not be able to identify the juveniles in the same manner as adults.

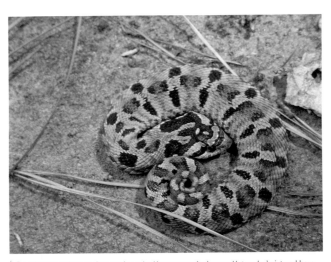

Fig. 2. Many harmless snakes, such as the Hognose snake (genus *Heterodon*) pictured here, can be mistaken for venomous ones. Photo by Tom Sinclair

An additional complicating factor in identification occurs when a snake's markings are temporarily obscured, making recognition more difficult. Approximately ten days before snakes shed their skins, the eyes and color pattern appear milky and opaque (the so-called "blue" phase), clearing again a few days before they shed. During this period, when the snake's pattern and colors are dulled, identification may not be easy. Incidentally, venomous snakes are generally more irritable than usual at this time and may be more prone to strike, since they are essentially blind and may be physiologically stressed. Consider also that snakes with abnormal features of color and pattern—including all-white specimens, all-yellow ones, or those that are completely black—sometimes occur among populations of normal-looking individuals. Such aberrant individuals are rare; even so, the more you familiarize yourself with the normal colors, markings, and overall appearance of a species, the easier it will be to recognize the occasional abnormally pigmented specimen.

VENOM

Snake venoms are complex substances, containing a large number of proteins with multiple lethal enzyme fractions, the specific composition of which varies among species and sometimes among individuals within a species (see, for example, the accounts for the timber rattlesnake and the Mojave rattlesnake). The importance of understanding the effects of specific enzyme components of venom, along with being able to identify the venomous species that occur naturally in Texas, cannot be overemphasized in the management and treatment of snakebite. Among lethal venom components are the following: neurotoxins, which interfere with the chemical communication between nerve cells (and thus nerve function) or between nerves (including those responsible for regulating breathing) and muscle cells at neuromuscular junctions, and which usually cause death from asphyxiation; proteolytic enzymes, which destroy blood-plasma proteins such as those involved in blood clotting, as well as collagen and other elastic connective tissues, the destruction of which results in local tissue damage (digestion); myonecrotic enzymes, which specifically destroy the functional microanatomy of muscles, perhaps through a massive disruption of the ability of the sarcolemma (the membrane surrounding a muscle) to regulate the influx of sodium ions, and through the disruption of ion-regulation functions in general; hemorrhagic enzymes, which cause blood to leak through vessel walls, and hemolytic enzymes, which destroy red blood cells, the effects of both of which reduce blood pressure and disrupt the delivery of oxygen to tissues; cardiovascular enzymes, which specifically attack heart muscle, decreasing cardiac output and perturbing blood pressure ratios; and cytolytic enzymes, which disrupt cellular function and destroy other cells in the body. Several major enzyme constituents of snake venom, such as phospholipase A2, may be present in multiple isoforms (functionally similar forms) in the venom of a particular species or an individual snake, each isoform contributing to one of the major lethal effects just outlined.

Individual snakes possess a limited quantity of venom at any one time, and what they have is energetically expensive to make. This may help explain why little or no venom is injected in 20%–40% of human venomous-snakebite cases in Texas ("dry bites"); venom is a precious commodity, since it is the primary means whereby a snake obtains a meal, and a snake is not going to waste it on anything else unless absolutely necessary. If venom is injected, the yield and toxicity depend on a number of variables: for the snake, these include the time interval since it last expended venom (which can take up to four days to resynthesize); the snake's age, size, and general health; environmental and seasonal effects; geographic location; and individual variation (genetic effects). Many of these same factors are also important in determining the outcome of a venomous snakebite for a victim. A given snakebite is likely to be more serious for the very young or very old, or for someone whose physiology is already compromised by disease or illness. In addition, the location of the bite on the body is important: bites on the extremities are less life-threatening and more easily treated than those closer to or on the trunk. The most important factor in the seriousness of a venomous snakebite, however, is the timeliness and quality of medical care provided to the victim.

Table 2, taken from Russell (1983), illustrates the variation just discussed.

SNAKEBITE

Texas snakes, including the venomous ones, are successful components of the ecosystems to which they belong; their ability to remain inconspicuous to potential enemies, including humans, is a part of this success. Sensing danger, a snake that is awake and alert is more likely to move off without first being detected by the average person outdoors. Failing that, a snake is most likely to remain hidden or stationary and to rely upon crypsis (camouflage) or threatening behavior, such as striking with a closed mouth, vibrating the tail, flattening or inflating the body, hissing, or rattling (in the case of rattlesnakes). Only from an acute sense of danger is a snake likely to bite. On the other hand, any snake is likely to bite if startled or surprised, such as if stepped on while asleep; in such cases, rattlesnakes are likely to bite without rattling first. Although snakebite is an unlikely event, it just makes sense to have a contingency plan: prior planning can be the most important contribution to surviving a venomous snakebite.

Precautions:

1. Learn to recognize the snakes that are likely to occur in the area in which you are or will be. This can have important consequences should treatment be necessary, and can render unnecessary the killing of harmless snakes.
2. Minimize the chances for an unfortunate encounter with a venomous snake by learning about their habits, when and where they are likely to be active, and under what conditions they are likely to strike.
3. Be sensible. Don't walk around after dark in snake country collecting firewood or engaging in other activities without a light. Check before putting your hands or feet in places that might conceal a snake. Don't sit down on the ground without inspecting the area nearby. Don't crawl beneath fences without first looking underneath them carefully. Don't sleep

TABLE 2. Percentage of victims exhibiting various symptoms from rattlesnake bites

SYMPTOM	PERCENTAGE OF VICTIMS AFFECTED
Fang marks	100
Swelling and edema	74
Weakness	70
Numbness or tingling of tongue, mouth, scalp, or feet	63
Changes in pulse rate	60
Faintness or dizziness	57
Tingling or numbing of affected part	57
Blood pressure changes	54
Ecchymosis	51
Sweating or chills	43
Nausea, vomiting, or both	42
Change in body temperature	42
Decreased blood platelets	42
Fasciculations	41
Respiratory rate changes	40
Vesiculations	40
Swelling of regional lymph nodes	40
Increased blood clotting time	37
Decreased hemoglobin	37
Thirst	34
Pain, necrosis	27
Abnormal electrocardiogram	26
Glycosuria	20
Increased salivation	20
Sphering of red blood cells	18
Cyanosis	16
Proteinuria	16
Hematemesis, hematuria, or melena	15
Unconsciousness	12
Blurring of vision	12
Swollen eyelids	7
Muscle contractions	6
Retinal hemorrhage	5
Increased blood platelets	4
Convulsions	1

Note: *Adapted from Russell 1983.*

near wood or rubbish piles, at the entrance to a cave, or near swampy areas.

4. Be careful. Dress appropriately; wear boots, shoes, long pants, or other protective clothing where encounters are likely. A normal defensive strike by a pit viper at ground level is unlikely to penetrate boots or canvas pants, and a number of "snakeproof" leggings are commercially available.

5. Be smart. Don't play around with live or dead venomous snakes; "dead" ones have been known to bite and inject venom. Physicians emphasize that approximately half of the bites treated annually are "illegitimate"; that is, they result from interactions between humans and snakes that are premeditated by the former.

6. Be prepared. Know what to do (and not to do) when engaging in activities where encounters with venomous snakes are a possibility.

FIRST AID

Recommended measures:

1. Assume envenomation has occurred, especially if initial symptoms are present. Initial symptoms of pit viper bites include fang puncture marks (Fig. 3) and almost always include immediate burning pain at the bite site, immediate and usually progressive local swelling within five minutes, and local discoloration of the skin (ecchymosis) due to the destruction of blood vessels and red blood cells. Initial symptoms of coral snake bites include tremors, slurred speech, blurred or double vision, drowsiness or euphoria, and a marked increase in salivation within four hours; however, life-threatening effects from coral snake envenomation may not be evident for twenty-four hours or longer.

2. Identifying the species of venomous snake inflicting the bite may provide useful information for emergency medical personnel attempting to judge the onset and severity of symptoms, but is not necessary to ensure proper clinical treatment.

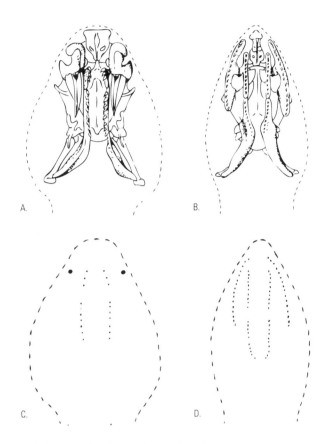

Fig. 3. Bite patterns (*modified from Pope and Perkins 1944*).

A. Upper jaw of a pit viper viewed from below, showing the two fangs and the two parallel rows of smaller teeth between them.

B. Upper jaw of bull snake (nonvenomous) viewed from below, showing the four rows of small teeth.

C. Typical pit viper bite pattern. Note the two large fang punctures (smaller rows of tooth punctures may or may not be present).

D. Typical nonvenomous snakebite pattern. Note the absence of two large fang punctures (incomplete bites occasionally result in omission of part of pattern).

Appropriate precautions should be taken in attempting to identify the snake in order to avoid another person being bitten.

3. Keep the victim as calm as possible. This helps reduce the spread of venom and delay the onset of shock to a stressed physiological system.

4. Keep yourself and any other members of the group calm as well. This will help reassure the victim and ensure that the appropriate first-aid measures are followed. It may also prevent anyone else from becoming injured.

5. Know and be alert for the symptoms of shock, and institute the proper treatment if it ensues. Respiratory distress or renal shutdown are frequent symptoms of envenomation.

6. Wash the bite area with a disinfectant, if available.

7. Remove jewelry such as rings and watches, as well as tight-fitting clothes, before the onset of swelling.

8. Reduce the movement of or immobilize a bitten extremity, using a splint if possible; this helps decrease the spread of venom. Position the extremity below the level of the heart for the same reason.

9. Get the victim to a medical facility as soon as possible and begin treatment there with intravenous (IV) antivenom, crystalloid solutions, and antibiotics. Antivenom treatment is generally most effective within the first four hours of envenomation and ineffective after eight to ten hours.

Measures absolutely to AVOID:

1. DO NOT make incisions over the bite marks. This can significantly damage already traumatized tissue, damage intact structures such as nerves and blood vessels, enhance bleeding caused by the anticoagulant components of venom, and enhance the rapid spread of venom throughout the body if the circulatory system is compromised. A suction device, such as the Sawyer Extractor/TM, may be used and may remove significant quantities of venom, although its efficacy is in question.

2. DO NOT use a tourniquet or other constricting band except in extreme cases of envenomation, and then only if properly trained in the technique. Such devices are of no value if applied more than thirty minutes after the bite, and if improperly used, they can restrict vital blood flow to the traumatized tissue and possibly result in the amputation of an extremity. Unbearable pain can also result, and the improper loosening of such devices can allow sudden systemic absorption of venom.

3. DO NOT use cryotherapy (including cold compresses, ice, dry ice, chemical ice packs, spray refrigerants, and freezing) for the same reasons as above and because it can increase the area of necrosis (dead tissue).

4. DO NOT use electroshock therapy, a method popularized following the publication of a letter from a missionary in South America, who reported its effectiveness in treating bites from snakes of uncertain identity. Several controlled clinical trials and at least one on humans have failed to demonstrate any positive result. The potential negative results from the uncontrolled use of an electric charge should be obvious.

5. DO NOT drink alcohol, since it dilates blood vessels and increases absorption from the circulatory system, and thus helps spread venom faster.

6. DO NOT use aspirin or similar medications to relieve pain, because they increase bleeding. A pain reliever not containing aspirin may be used.

7. DO NOT, when treating pit viper bites, use the pressure-immobilization technique, which consists of firmly wrapping the entire limb with an elastic bandage and then splinting. The theory behind this treatment is to confine the venom to the area of the bite until a medical facility is reached, but studies have shown the technique to be ineffective or worse with venoms that produce local swelling and tissue damage.

8. DO NOT administer antivenom in the field unless properly trained in the procedure, unless evacuation to a medical facility will take many hours or even days, or unless extreme

envenomation has occurred. Intramuscular (im) or subcutaneous (sc) application of antivenom has proved to be much less effective than IV administration, and in some cases even ineffective. Acute allergic reactions to antivenom can occur, and the contemplated field administration of antivenom should include provision for a sufficient supply of epinephrine (Adrenalin) to counteract any such effects.

MEDICAL TREATMENT

Long-term care and recovery, the details of which will vary in each case, are best left to the discretion of trained and experienced medical personnel. Patients may take several weeks to recover from severe envenomations, and symptoms may appear or recur anytime during this period, especially in cases in which antivenom therapy is contraindicated. The prognosis is generally good in cases of muscle or tissue damage, provided that blood circulation and nerve connections to the affected area remain good and infection doesn't set in. Surgery is generally not called for except to relieve intramuscular compartmental pressure from swelling. Antivenom therapy can be greatly enhanced through the use of specific enzyme immunoassays of the patient's blood and other body fluids. Secondary complications, such as kidney failure, hypotension (low blood pressure), or anaphylaxis (allergic shock), are common, and must be anticipated in treatment.

In cases of envenomation by coral snakes, antivenom therapy is only one component of successful treatment. Patients should be observed for at least twenty-four hours because paralysis from bites may not occur immediately. In cases of severe paralysis, only an endotracheal intubation with mechanical ventilation will save the patient, since administration of antivenom will not reverse paralysis. Pneumonia, brain damage, or death may result if ventilation is not performed quickly and appropriately; with proper ventilation, the neuromuscular blockade will gradually decrease and the patient will ultimately return to normal.

PIT VIPERS

All of the dangerously venomous snakes native to Texas, except one, are pit vipers: members of the subfamily Crotalinae (family Viperidae), although they are sometimes considered as belonging to their own family, the Crotalidae. There are roughly 160 species distributed widely throughout temperate and tropical Asia, North America, and South America. They share with the true vipers the unique rotating, hinged-fang venom delivery system, or solenoglyphy. Briefly, the maxillae, the major tooth-bearing bones on either side of the upper skull, are short and stout and bear no teeth other than the fangs. These are located on the anterior ends of the maxillae and are connected by ducts to the venom glands. The hollow fangs have an elongate opening on their anterior face, and are folded against the upper jaw along the roof of the mouth when not in use. Several skull bones are connected in a lever-and-pulley arrangement (Fig. 4), allowing each fang to pivot independently forward and downward (perpendicular to the jaw) during a strike.

A reserve fang series also exists; when a fang breaks or is shed, it is quickly replaced.

The major venom gland is located on each side of the head behind the eye and above the angle of the jaw. An accessory gland of unknown function is situated along the outer edge of the upper jaw just below and forward of each eye. The main gland is surrounded by muscles that contract to expel venom. These muscles are separate from the biting muscles, so snakes can control whether and how much venom is injected. This suite of adaptive characteristics allows vipers to kill much heavier and bulkier prey than other venomous snakes, lessens the risk of harm to the vipers from their prey, and has allowed for the evolution of a stout, robust body form.

Unlike true vipers, pit vipers possess specialized nerves that bear receptors sensitive to infrared radiation. Boas and pythons (families Boidae and Pythonidae) also possess such receptors. In the case of the pit vipers, the receptors are gathered together in small pit-like structures, the openings of which are located on each side of the face, between the eye and the nostril, and which give the group as a whole its vernacular name. These receptors pick up infrared radiation given off as body heat (by a small mammal, for example) and transmit this information to the snake's brain, which forms an image that overlaps with, and in some cases may be sharper than, that formed by the visual system. Infrared receptors are instrumental in guiding a pit viper's predatory strike.

All snakes use their tongues as a chemical-identification system, so when a snake flicks out its tongue, it is in a sense "smelling" its environment. Odor molecules are adsorbed onto the moist surface of the tongue and, when the snake retracts it, transferred to fleshy pads on the floor of the mouth. These pads in turn are pressed up against two small holes in the anterior roof of the mouth, which lead to a unique structure called the Jacobson's organ or, more generally, the vomeronasal organ (VNO). The VNO develops embryonically as an outpocketing of the nasal capsule, but becomes separated from it during development. The VNO is richly supplied with nerves that transmit chemical information to the brain. This sensory system is very precise, allowing snakes

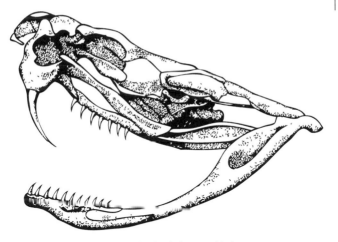

Fig. 4a. Side view of a pit viper skull, showing the long, movable fang.

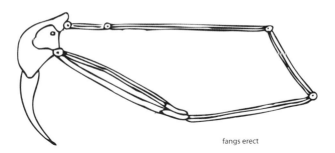

fangs erect

fangs retracted

Fig. 4b. Diagram of the poison apparatus of pit vipers, showing the lever-and-pulley arrangement of the skull bones _(from Klauber 1972)._

to discriminate the sexual identity and receptivity of others of their kind during the mating season, as well as to identify enemies and prey. The forked structure of the tongue provides a snake with feedback when following a chemical trail. As long as the stimulus intensity from both forks is approximately equal, the snake knows it is on the trail; if the stimulus on one side becomes stronger than on the other, the snake can correct by turning in the opposite direction until the signals are equal again. The VNO is a vital component of the feeding behavior of venomous snakes, like pit vipers, which release their prey after striking. It provides a snake with the unique chemical "signature" of its prey and allows the snake to find it, although it may have traveled several meters before its death.

Pit vipers have many natural enemies despite their venomous nature. Some of these have developed serum blood factors that convey a greater or lesser degree of immunity to pit viper venom. These factors are most effective against venoms with hemorrhagic or proteolytic actions, and ineffective against venoms with hypotensive peptides, neurotoxins, or myolytic phospholipases. Pit vipers in turn have evolved a most interesting defensive response when confronted by an attack from enemies immune to their venom, such as skunks or king snakes. Rather than exhibiting the classic posture of a coiled body with the head poised to strike, pit vipers will position their bodies between the attacker and their own head and tail. Then, one or more loops of the body are raised in the air and brought down in a clubbing motion directed at the attacker in an attempt to drive it off (Fig. 5). This peculiar behavior is elicited by specific chemical signals that the attackers possess and that pit vipers recognize through the VNO system described above.

All of the pit vipers native to Texas give birth to live young. A placenta-like structure is formed between the mother and the developing fetuses, and some degree of nutritional and waste exchange occurs across it. The young are born contained within a clear embryonic membrane from which they emerge within a minute or two. All pit vipers in Texas can be distinguished from other snakes by the combination of the facial pit openings, vertically elliptical pupils, and a single row of subcaudal scales (Fig. 6).

Genus *Agkistrodon*

The cosmopolitan snakes of the *Agkistrodon* complex, thirty-five species and subspecies in at least four genera, are considered to include some of the most primitive of the pit vipers. The name *Agkistrodon* is from a Greek combination meaning "hooked tooth," undoubtedly referring to the enlarged front fangs. The most recent evidence suggests that the genus itself originated in the New World, following the dispersal of ancient pit viper stock across the Bering land bridge during the Late Oligocene–Early

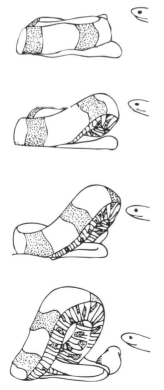

Fig. 5. Pit viper driving off an attacker by using a clubbing motion (*from Carpenter and Gillingham, 1975*).

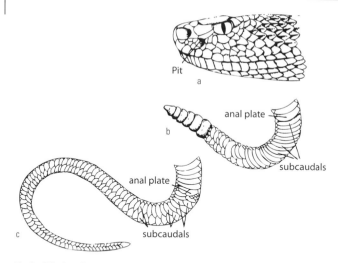

Fig. 6a. Side view of a typical pit-viper head, showing the facial pit and the elliptical pupil.

b. Underside of a representative pit-viper tail. Note the single row of subcaudals.

c. Underside of representative tail of most nonvenomous snakes and coral snakes. Note the double row of subcaudals.

Miocene transition (around 25 million years ago); diversification into the forms we recognize today took place by the end of the latter epoch. The current New World distribution includes the southeastern third of the United States, from southern New England westward to Kansas, extending in a disjunct fashion southward through Mexico, primarily along both coasts, to Costa Rica.

The two species of the genus that occur in Texas are as follows:

COPPERHEAD
Agkistrodon contortrix (Linnaeus, 1766)

CONTENT Five subspecies are recognized. Three of these occur in Texas: the southern copperhead (*A. c. contortrix*), the broad-banded copperhead (*A. c. laticinctus*), and the Trans-Pecos copperhead (*A. c. pictigaster*).

DESCRIPTION Copperheads are medium-sized, relatively robust pit vipers, with adult males typically 1.5–2 feet (45–60 cm) in length, and females somewhat smaller. The largest verifiable record for the forms that occur in Texas was of an individual 4 feet 4 inches (1.32 m) in length. Usually 23 (21–25) scale rows are present at midbody (in the Trans-Pecos copperhead, this figure is likely to be 21 or 22); dorsal scales are moderately to weakly keeled but

Fig. 7. Southern copperhead (_Agkistrodon contortrix contortrix_). Photo by Mike Price

Fig. 8. Broad-banded copperhead (_Agkistrodon contortrix laticinctus_). Photo by Mike Price

Fig. 9. Trans-Pecos copperhead (*Agkistrodon contortrix pictigaster*). Photo by Mike Price

may be smooth, especially toward the front of the body. Ventrals number 138–156, with little sexual dimorphism; subcaudals number 37–62, with males averaging about 3 more than females. Subcaudals may show a tendency to be divided, especially toward the tail tip and in western populations. There are 9 symmetrically arranged plates anteriorly on top of the head, followed by numerous smaller scales.

The ground color in the southern copperhead is pale tan to reddish tan, somewhat darker toward the midline. The top of the head is unmarked except for a small dark spot on each parietal scale. The face below the eyes and backward to the angle of the jaw is pale gray to silver gray in color, and is bordered by a darker postocular stripe with a distinct lower border and a diffuse upper border. The dorsal pattern consists of 10–18 reddish brown hourglass-shaped markings, darker toward their margins, which are narrow along the spine and wider on the sides. They have a tendency not to meet along the spine, where a pair may in fact be offset, creating a somewhat mosaic appearance. These dorsal markings do not reach the ventral scales, which are unmarked except for a series of more or less distinct dark blotches along their outer margins.

In the broad-banded copperhead, the dorsal ground color is pale brown with a fine stippling of red, gray, or black. The dorsal bands are wide and usually complete, dark brown to red brown, usually with narrow light borders, and extend to and usually across the ventral scales.

The dorsal color hues of the Trans-Pecos copperhead are somewhat richer, and often the head is brighter than the remainder of the body. The black belly blotches are expanded, fuse across the midline, and extend onto the lower sides of the body, where they blend into the middle of the light dorsal body bands at their lower margins. The tail tip is bright yellow in newborns of all subspecies, fading with age.

DIFFERENTIATING SIMILAR SPECIES Rattlesnakes (genera *Crotalus* and *Sistrurus*) have a rattle (even just a button) on the end of their tails. Cottonmouths (*Agkistrodon piscivorus*) are generally darker, have a more pointed snout, may possess a light band from below the eye backward to the angle of the mouth, and lack a loreal scale. Harmless colubrid snakes lack the facial pit and usually have rounded pupils and patterned heads; if elliptical pupils are present, as in the night snakes and lyre snakes (genera *Hypsiglena* and *Trimorphodon*), then there is usually some type of pattern on the top of the head.

HABITAT Copperheads occupy a wide variety of wooded habitats, from the hardwood bottomlands along major rivers in East Texas to willow-oak-walnut-hackberry woodlands, which often exist as isolated patches, in the Trans-Pecos. They can be found in open habitats such as vacant lots, old fields, and other agricultural or suburban locations that are not too far from wooded habitats. The natural range of this species extends into drier habitats only along wooded watercourses or other similar corridors, such as the Cross Timbers in north-central Texas.

BEHAVIOR Copperheads are relatively shy and inoffensive unless provoked by being stepped on, prodded, or otherwise disturbed. Copperheads do occasionally climb, but spend most of their time on the ground. Although partial to moist microhabitats and able to swim, they are rarely found in the water. While waiting for prey or digesting a meal, individual snakes may remain loosely coiled for several days in the same spot under a log or similar object, in the open at the base of a tree, on a rocky ledge, or at the edge of a patch of vegetation. Their color pattern provides superb camouflage in these conditions, and most copperheads go undetected by the unobservant. Copperheads may be active throughout the year under suitable environmental conditions. They are generally active during the day in spring and fall, and switch to nocturnal activity during the summer, when daytime temperatures become too warm. Copperheads will cease being surface-active during the winter if they cannot maintain body temperatures above 50°F (10°C), and they cannot tolerate body temperatures much above 77°F (25°C) during the summer.

REPRODUCTION Mating behavior in this species is very similar to that described for the western diamondback rattlesnake. Males physically compete with one another for access to receptive females, and females may actively reject suitors defeated in such contests. Mating in Texas occurs most frequently in the spring or the fall, but can occur any time snakes are active. Females mating in the fall will not give birth until the following year, and some females store viable sperm for at least two years. Females attain sexual maturity at a minimum of 3 years of age and about 18.5 inches (47 cm) in total length, but this can vary between individuals and is dependent on their ability to sequester sufficient energy reserves to support breeding activity. Pregnant females are largely sedentary, and may aggregate to give birth. Litter size ranges from two to fifteen, and is positively correlated with body size. Young are born in August and September and are about 6–8 inches (16–20 cm) in body length.

PREY AND PREDATORS Copperheads are extremely catholic in their diets, eating a wide variety of vertebrates and invertebrates. Prey selection is size-based, with larger snakes eating larger prey items. Prey are hunted by ambush or by careful stalking behavior, and young copperheads may use their brightly colored tail tips to lure prey within striking distance. Animals known to have been eaten by copperheads in Texas include the Mexican free-tailed bat,

Fig. 10. Southern copperhead with offspring. Photo by Tom Sinclair

deer mouse, white-throated sparrow, green anole, common five-lined skink, little brown skink, long-nosed snake, western ribbon snake, rough earth snake, mottled rock rattlesnake, cliff chirping frog, and cicada. In neighboring Arkansas and Louisiana, add the woodland vole, house mouse, cotton rat, least shrew, bullfrog, green frog, and southern leopard frog to the menu.

Copperheads themselves, especially young ones, fall victim to a wide variety of predators. In Texas, known predators include raccoons, Virginia opossums, gray foxes, ringtails, and reptiles (common king snakes and coral snakes). Evidence suggests that copperheads were occasionally eaten by Native Americans, especially during times of relative food shortage.

VENOM CHARACTERISTICS Adult venom yields are typically 40–72 mg, with a maximum recorded yield of 148 mg (dry weight). Larger snakes produce more venom. Published LD_{50} values range 6.5–10.5 mg/kg (ip), 10.92 mg/kg (iv), and 20.2–26.1 mg/kg (sc). The lethal human dose is unknown but has been estimated at 100 mg or more, with less than 0.5% of bites resulting in fatalities. Bites from this species should be taken seriously, but are generally not considered life-threatening, because of the small yields and reduced lethality of the venom. There are very few differences in venom characteristics between the subspecies. This venom induces less hemolytic activity than that of cottonmouths. Copperheads possess blood-serum factors that render them immune to their own venom and that of cottonmouths.

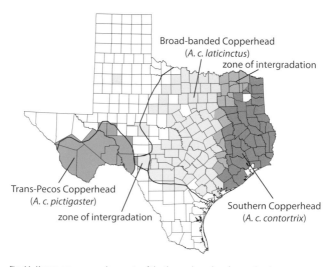

Fig. 11. Known occurrences, by county, of the three subspecies of copperhead.

FOSSIL RECORD The fossil record of this species in Texas is as follows (by county): Pliocene (Scurry), Pleistocene (Hardeman, Kendall, Lubbock), Recent/Archaic (Bexar, Freestone, Goliad, Jackson, Live Oak, Navarro, Travis, Val Verde, Williamson).

REMARKS Males grow faster than females after about 3 years of age and reach a larger average size. The maximum lifespan documented for individuals of the 3 subspecies occurring in Texas exceeds 20 years in captivity, but copperheads in the wild rarely live past 10 years of age. The specimen record for Lubbock County, outside the natural range of the species, resulted from an individual found within a load of cedar fence posts from Kerrville.

The name *contortrix* (Latin) means "twisting" or "twister" and probably refers to the dorsal pattern; the name *laticinctus* (Latin) means "broad band," again referring to the dorsal pattern; the name *pictigaster* (Latin) means "painted belly" and refers to the extensive pigmentation found in this subspecies.

COTTONMOUTH
Agkistrodon piscivorus (Lacepede, 1789)

CONTENT Three subspecies are recognized; the western cottonmouth (*A. p. leucostoma*) occurs in Texas.

DESCRIPTION Cottonmouths are medium-sized stout-bodied pit vipers, with adult males typically 20–30 inches (50–76 cm) in length, and females somewhat smaller. The largest verifiable record for this subspecies is of an individual 5 feet 2 inches (1.57 m) in length. Usually 25 scale rows are present at midbody; the lowermost scales may be only weakly keeled, and apical pits are present. Ventrals number 128–142, with little sexual dimorphism. Subcaudals number 36–53, with males averaging about 3 more than females, and show a tendency to be divided toward the tip of the tail. There are 9 symmetrically arranged plates anteriorly on top of the head, followed by numerous smaller scales.

The dorsal ground color is light to dark brown, and many adults are black. There are 10–15 complete or incomplete crossbands in patterned individuals, varying from only slightly darker than the

Fig. 12. Western cottonmouth (*Agkistrodon piscivorus leucostoma*). Photo by Mike Price

ground color to black and forming a series of spots where they extend onto the ventral surface. The ventral surface is otherwise pale and immaculate except anteriorly, where it may be black. The head is brown or black, generally unmarked, and possesses a more or less distinct white stripe that extends backward from a point below the eye to the angle of the mouth. The pattern of newborn and juvenile snakes is sharp and distinct and fades with age, as does the light green or yellow color of the tail.

DIFFERENTIATING SIMILAR SPECIES Rattlesnakes (genus *Crotalus* and *Sistrurus*) have a rattle (even just a button) on the end of the tail. Copperheads (*Agkistrodon contortrix*) are generally light brown to reddish brown in color, have a more rounded snout, lack a light band below the eye backward to the angle of the mouth, and have a loreal scale. Harmless colubrid snakes lack the facial pit and usually have rounded pupils and patterned heads; if they have elliptical pupils, as in the night snakes and lyre snakes (genera *Hypsiglena* and *Trimorphodon*), then there is usually some pattern present on the top of the head. Harmless water snakes (genus *Nerodia*), which are routinely mistaken for cottonmouths, can readily be distinguished on the basis of color, pattern, and behavior. Water snakes have eyes that protrude beyond the supraocular scale, whereas the eyes of cottonmouths do not, giving them a "scowling" look.

HABITAT Cottonmouths occupy a wide variety of aquatic and semi-aquatic habitats, and are most abundant where prey are plentiful and environmental temperatures are not too extreme. They can be found in salt marshes, ponds, swamps and bayous, river bottomlands, and streams that vary from muddy and sluggish to clear and fast-running. They require abundant basking sites, such as logs, brush piles, and mud banks, and they also do well in urban and reclaimed areas. Cottonmouths occur along major rivers, such as the Brazos and Colorado and their tributaries, and upstream into areas that are otherwise too hot and dry to support them.

BEHAVIOR Much is made of the aggressiveness of cottonmouths, but in truth their disposition is similar to that of copperheads. Fleeing is by far the most common defensive behavior, followed by

Fig. 13. Comparison of the western cottonmouth with harmless water snakes.

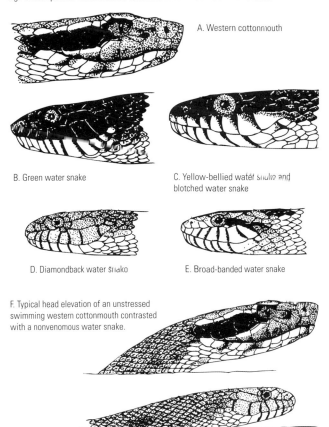

A. Western cottonmouth

B. Green water snake

C. Yellow-bellied water snake and blotched water snake

D. Diamondback water snake

E. Broad-banded water snake

F. Typical head elevation of an unstressed swimming western cottonmouth contrasted with a nonvenomous water snake.

mouth gaping, tail vibration, and the emission of musk from the anal scent glands. Striking is the least utilized response, occurring only during extreme provocation. Aggressiveness varies inversely with body size, therefore smaller (that is, younger) snakes are more likely to engage in and exhibit the most active defensive behaviors. Additionally, little or no venom is expended during these strikes. Preferred body temperatures for activity lie between 64°F and 84°F (18-29°C). They are good swimmers, but sluggish on land. When

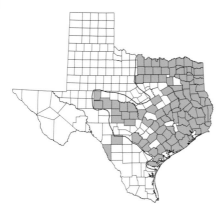

Fig. 14. Known occurrences, by county, of the western cottonmouth (*Agkistrodon piscivorus leucostoma*).

not engaged in hunting or reproductive activities, cottonmouths spend much of their time coiled at the edge of bodies of water or draped loosely in overhanging vegetation, often asleep. When disturbed in such circumstances, their first response is to drop into the water as quickly as possible; stories of cottonmouths ending up in canoes or johnboats are most likely due to these vessels blocking the intended escape route. Cottonmouths on land and away from a convenient escape route often give the defensive display that earned this species its common name. The head is held at the center of the coiled body, and the mouth is gaped wide, revealing the milky white interior (harmless water snakes also have white mouths, but do not exhibit this behavior). Often the tail is vigorously vibrated, and a pungent musk emitted from scent glands at its base. Cottonmouths may travel far from water to hibernate.

REPRODUCTION Typical male courtship behavior consists of jerky body movements when trailing the female, rapid flicking of his tongue or rubbing his chin on her back, and repeated attempts at copulation while coiling his tail around hers. Courtship may occur in the water, and courting males on land may challenge intruding males with characteristic viperid dominance displays (the so-called "combat dance"). Mating in Texas probably occurs in the spring, but may take place at any time during the active season. Females probably attain sexual maturity at a minimum age of 3 years and a body length of 18–20 inches (45–50 cm). Young are born alive in late summer (July–September). Litter size ranges from four to eight babies, the number very much dependent on the size (and thus the overall health) of the mother. A mother may remain with her young for several days, until they shed their skin for the first time.

PREY AND PREDATORS On the menu for Texas snakes are the nutria, eastern mole, rice rat, fulvous harvest mouse, long-tailed weasel, northern pygmy mouse, hispid pocket mouse, least shrew, black-bellied whistling duck, white-winged dove, eastern meadowlark, brown-headed cowbird, American sparrows, northern mocking-bird, painted bunting, lark sparrow, American coot, red-winged blackbird, sora rail, flicker, northern cardinal, and purple gallinule. Reptiles and amphibians eaten include the corn snake, yellow-bellied king snake, plain-bellied water snake, brown water snake, western ribbon snake, western diamondback rattlesnake, lesser siren, green tree frog, and southern leopard frog. Catfish and cicadas are also taken. Additional prey items taken from snakes collected just across the Red River in Oklahoma include the hispid pocket mouse, Carolina chickadee, and bullfrog. Prey selection is size-based, with larger snakes eating larger prey items. Hunting is by ambush or by careful stalking behavior. Young cottonmouths have bright yellow or green tail tips, which they employ, in a stereotyped behavior pattern called "caudal luring," to attract food items. Juvenile snakes remain motionless except for the tail tip, which is undulated back and forth like a worm or an insect larva. Potential prey such as small lizards and frogs can be lured within striking distance.

Cottonmouths themselves, especially young ones, fall victim to a wide variety of predators, including alligators, other snakes (racers, king snakes), and birds such as herons and egrets. Dining on them in Texas are the great blue heron, whooping crane, Virginia opossum, and raccoon, and in Louisiana, the American alligator and common king snake. They may have occasionally been eaten by Native Americans, especially during times of food shortages.

VENOM CHARACTERISTICS Relatively little is known about the venom of this species. Adult venom yields are typically 90–170 mg dry weight. Published LD_{50} values include 5.11 mg/kg (ip), 4.00–4.17 mg/kg (iv), and 25.1 mg/kg (sc). The lethal human dose is unknown and undoubtedly variable, but has been estimated at 100–150 mg. Cottonmouth venom differs from copperhead venom in possessing considerable hemolytic properties.

FOSSIL RECORD The fossil record of this species in Texas is as follows (by county): Pleistocene (Denton, Kendall); Recent/Archaic (Chambers, Freestone, Goliad, Navarro, San Patricio, Zavala).

REMARKS Maximum lifespan for a captive individual of the Texas subspecies exceeded 21 years; natural life spans are probably similar to those of copperheads. The name *piscivorus* (Latin) means "fish eating," given to this species because of its dietary characteristics. The name *leucostoma* (Latin) means "white mouth," in reference to the feature that earned this species its common name.

Rattlesnakes

Rattlesnakes are typical animals of the natural landscape of Texas, represented by at least one species in almost every county. They have appeared relatively recently on the evolutionary stage as a group, with the oldest known fossils dating from the Pliocene (4–12 million years ago). There are two groups of rattlesnakes. The more primitive forms belong to the genus *Sistrurus* (three species, two in Texas), and are characterized by a series of nine plates on the crown of the head. This genus is distributed throughout the southeastern quarter of the United States, with disjunct populations in central Mexico. The more advanced forms of rattlesnakes belong to the genus *Crotalus* (at least twenty-eight species, six in Texas), which have small scales covering the crown of the head (Fig. 15). This genus occurs from Canada to Argentina, including a number of islands in the Sea of Cortez and off the northern coast of South America. All but one rattlesnake species (an isolated island form in the Sea of Cortez) possess the rattle in addition to the characteristic features mentioned earlier for pit vipers. Both generic names are derived from Greek and refer to the possession of rattles on the tail.

Fig. 15. Comparison of scales

 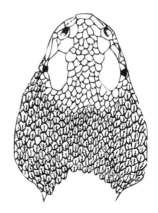

A. *Sistrurus* (also *Agkistrodon*).   B. *Crotalus*.

The rattle is a series of hollow, loosely interlocking segments of keratin, basically the same material that forms fingernails. The contraction of a series of specialized muscles in the tail, called shaker muscles, causes these segments to vibrate against one another. The sound produced is amplified because the segments are hollow, and the intensity and other acoustic properties of the sound are dependent upon the size of the rattle. A rattlesnake's age cannot be determined from the number of segments of its rattle, since a new segment is added with each shedding of the snake's skin. Snakes shed their skins as part of the growth process, and will shed more often when they are younger and when food is plentiful. An individual rattlesnake may thus shed its skin 4–6 times annually during the first several years of life, and perhaps only once a year after reaching maturity. In addition, segments are frequently broken off as individuals traverse their environment, so an older rattlesnake with a complete rattle is rarely seen. If all the rattle segments were to be lost through an accident, a rattlesnake's tail would end in a stump rather than a gradually tapered point, as is characteristic of all other snakes.

Texas rattlesnakes are as follows:

WESTERN DIAMONDBACK RATTLESNAKE
Crotalus atrox (Baird and Girard, 1853)

CONTENT No subspecies have been recognized.

DESCRIPTION Western diamondbacks are large rattlesnakes, with adults typically ranging from 2.5 to 4.5 feet (76–137 cm) in total length. The maximum recorded size is a male from Dallas County, Texas, at 7 feet 8 inches (2.34 m) in total length. Adult males are about 10% larger than females of the same age. There are 23–29 (usually 25) keeled scale rows at midbody. Males have 168–193 ventral scales and 19–32 subcaudals; corresponding counts in females are 173–196 and 16–36. There are 11–32 small scales on the crown of the head between the snout and the eyes, and 3–8 intersupraocular scales.

The ground color is brown to gray, although certain populations may be reddish, yellowish, or blackish, depending on the prevailing substrate. The dorsal pattern consists of 24–45 dark diamond-shaped markings or irregular hexagons with light borders that are somewhat indistinct because their scales are not uniform in color. A series of indistinct lateral dark markings extends along each side. The tail is distinctly marked with black and white bands (thus

Fig. 16. Western diamondback rattlesnake (*Crotalus atrox*). Photo by Mike Price

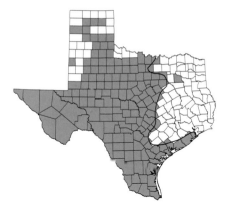

Fig. 17. Known occurrences, by county, of the western diamondback rattlesnake (*Crotalus atrox*).

the vernacular name, "coontail") that are approximately equal in width and number 4–16. A pair of distinct white stripes, one from in front of and one from behind the eye, extend downward and backward to the mouth; the posterior stripe makes contact well in front of the angle of the jaw. Albino individuals and some with normal ground color but lacking a dorsal pattern altogether or with only a narrow dark stripe along the spine have been found occasionally in Bexar, Haskell, and Travis counties.

DIFFERENTIATING SIMILAR SPECIES The species in Texas most likely to be confused with this one is the Mojave rattlesnake. That species has larger scales on the top of the head (1–2, rarely 3 intersupraoculars), black tail bands that are usually much narrower than the white ones, a posterior white stripe on the side of the head extending backward above the angle of the mouth, a border of light unicolored scales around each dorsal blotch (making the pattern very distinct), and the last half of the basal rattle segment paler than the first half. Hybridization between the two species does occur in the Big Bend, and hybrid individuals may exhibit one or more characteristics that are intermediate between the two.

HABITAT This species can be found in virtually every dry-land habitat within its range, although it seems to prefer habitats that are neither too closed (e.g., dense woodland) nor too open (e.g., shortgrass prairie). Habitats in which western diamondbacks may be especially abundant include rocky canyons, such as those cutting into the caprock escarpment of the Panhandle, the Edwards and Stockton plateaus of west-central Texas, the creosote-bush deserts of far West Texas, the mesquite savannahs of South Texas, and the dunes and coastal barrier islands along the Gulf Coast. Caves are also frequently used for shelter from the elements as well as hibernacula.

BEHAVIOR Western diamondbacks are active all year long in southern Texas; in more northern populations, individuals that overwinter in dens may be active around them for extended periods on warm days. Western diamondbacks typically leave their winter dens in March–May, when daylong temperatures become warm enough, and migrate to their summer ranges. Migration distances can be up to several kilometers, and home ranges as large as twenty-two acres (nine hectares). During the warm summer months, western diamondbacks are active largely at night, although they may continue their activity into early morning hours, before it gets too hot. Preferred body temperatures for activity are 75–86°F (24–30°C). As day length shortens and nighttime temperatures cool in the late summer, western diamondbacks increase their proportion of daytime activity and begin their migration to winter den sites. The mechanisms by which they navigate are largely unknown, but are thought to involve chemical and solar cues along with geographic landmarks.

When disturbed, these snakes are quick to assume the well-known defensive posture immortalized in the minds of so many generations of people through books, stories, movies, and TV shows as well as the postcards found in virtually every traveler's stop in western America. The striking pose has the head and front part of the body held high and retracted in an S-shaped coil directly over the rest of the body, which is anchored firmly to the ground. The rattle is shaken vigorously, and the tongue is extended repeatedly, often held in place for a second or two while curved backward over the top of the head. A snake can maintain this posture seemingly indefinitely if it continues to perceive a threat to its safety. It is important to recognize this behavior as being strictly defensive on the part of the snake, however; should the threat not escalate (for example, if the threatening object stands still or retreats), the intensity of the display will slowly diminish and the snake will move away to seek safety.

REPRODUCTION Mating most often takes place in the spring, following emergence from winter hibernation, but may also occur throughout the summer and into the fall. A male actively courts a female, using tactile and chemical cues as it slowly approaches her, rubs its chin along her back while flicking its tongue rapidly, and exhibits precise body movements. Females will move off if not ready to mate, but if receptive, they will move very little, and the actual copulation may last for as long as twenty-four hours. The mating season is also the time when snake "dancing" is observed. This behavior involves two snakes raising the front halves of their bodies off the ground and twisting them together (Fig. 18). These "dances" almost always involve two males engaged in a struggle for dominance, whether or not a female is actually present.

Females attain sexual maturity at three years of age and at about 3 feet (90 cm) in length. Diamondbacks in northern and central Texas may reproduce only once every two years, whereas those in southern Texas may do so annually. Litter size is correlated with female body size, and averages about 14 young, with a maximum of 25 reported. They are born from July through September, again depending on geographic location. Neonates are about 14 inches (36 cm) in total length and grow rapidly during their first year; most growth occurs during the first four years of life. Individual females may travel long distances from their summer ranges to give birth, and are known to remain near their newborns for up to a week, at least until the young shed their skins for the first time.

PREY AND PREDATORS Larger snakes prefer prey such as cottontails, ground squirrels, wood rats, and kangaroo rats, whereas smaller individuals take smaller prey, such as pocket mice, white-footed mice, and harvest mice. Small birds and lizards are occasionally eaten. When prey is scarce, dead animals may be scavenged, and snakes can go for extended periods of time without eating at all.

Many prey species have been documented in Texas, including the Mexican free-tailed bat, black-tailed jackrabbit, cottontail, swamp rabbit, desert cottontail, least shrew, hispid cotton rat, white-throated wood rat, southern plains wood rat, deer mouse,

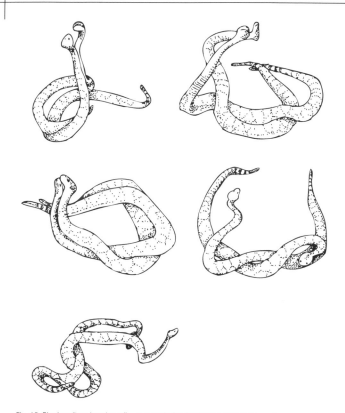

Fig. 18. Pit viper "combat dance"—a struggle for dominance. During the mating season, two males rear upward and twist together until one is pushed against the ground (*from Shaw and Campbell, 1974*).

harvest mouse, Mexican vole, northern pygmy mouse, plains pocket mouse, hispid pocket mouse, Nelson's pocket mouse, desert pocket mouse, Merriam's pocket mouse, silky pocket mouse, kangaroo rats, plains pocket gopher, fox squirrel, Mexican ground squirrel, rock squirrel, Old World rats, black skimmer, Caspian tern, laughing gull, Wilson's plover, white-winged dove, northern bobwhite, scaled quail, eastern towhee, northern mockingbird, song sparrow, lazuli bunting, indigo bunting, Texas banded gecko, reticulate collared lizard, earless lizards, Texas horned lizard, spiny lizards, common side-blotched lizard, whiptail lizards, four-lined skink, and cliff chirping frog. A brown rat was observed in combat with a two-foot snake, which the rat eventually killed, in Travis County; who was the predator and whom the prey is uncertain.

In Texas, the Virginia opossum, domestic cat, bobcat, ocelot (possibly), feral hog, crested caracara, white-tailed hawk, wild turkey, roadrunner, domestic chicken, indigo snake, common king snake, and coachwhip are known predators. A white-tailed deer was reported to have killed a rattlesnake by repeatedly jumping on it with its front hooves. Coyotes are known to exhibit aversion behavior toward objects painted with secretions from scent glands in the base of the tail.

Evidence shows that these snakes were regularly eaten by Native Americans and occasionally by European settlers.

VENOM CHARACTERISTICS Adult venom yields are large, averaging 400 mg (dry weight), with a maximum recorded of 1,150 mg. The fangs are relatively long (.4–.5 inches [10–13 mm] in adults). Average IP LD_{50} values (mg/kg) have been shown to vary from 1.0 in young (eight months old) to 5.0 (3.7–8.4) in adults. Other published LD_{50} ranges are 3.71–13.6 (ip), 1.0–6.3 (iv), and 16–19 (sc) mg/kg. The average lethal human dose is unknown and undoubtedly variable, but has been estimated at approximately 100 mg of venom. Western diamondback venom possesses high proteolytic and anticoagulant activity, but individuals of this species possess blood-borne factors that confer immunity to the hemorrhagic effects of conspecific venom. A number of potential predator and prey species, including opossums, raccoons, wood rats, ground squirrels, and white-tailed hawks, possess similar factors that confer varying degrees of immunity. There is some indication to suggest that older snakes produce less toxic venom.

FOSSIL RECORD The fossil record of this species in Texas is as follows (by county): Pliocene (Scurry); Pleistocene (Bexar, Brewster, Denton, Mason, Lubbock, Val Verde, Victoria); Recent/Historic (Bexar, Coke, Concho, Culberson, Dallas, Delta, DeWitt, El Paso, Ellis, Goliad, Gonzales, Hays, Hidalgo, Hill, Jackson, Jim Wells, Kerr, Live Oak, Maverick, McLennan, McMullen, Montague, Nueces, San Patricio, Tarrant, Terrell, Tom Green, Travis, Uvalde,

Val Verde, Victoria, Willacy, Williamson, Wilson, Zavala). Many of these sites are associated with areas of Native American occupation, and western diamondbacks were sometimes used as food. This species also occasionally provided artifacts, such as a necklace made of vertebrae, for prehistoric Native American burials in Texas.

REMARKS Captive individuals have lived as long as thirty years. Annual mortality in the wild is reported to be about 20%; rarely, individuals may live to be fifteen years old. The name *atrox* (Latin) means "savage," "fierce," or "cruel," probably in reference to its imposing defensive display and venomous nature, and to the reactions of nineteenth-century settlers and explorers who first encountered this species.

Free-ranging Japanese macaques in South Texas have learned to recognize western diamondbacks as potential predators and have developed warning signals among members of the troop.

I quote a paper from the turn of the twentieth century: "The oil [of the rattlesnake] makes a fine foundation for a linement [*sic*], and is used by old ranchmen on sorebacked horses; and it is claimed to be a specific for rheumatism."

TIMBER RATTLESNAKE
Crotalus horridus (Linnaeus, 1758)

CONTENT No subspecies are recognized (see Remarks, below).
DESCRIPTION Timber rattlesnakes are large rattlesnakes, with adult males averaging about 4 feet 3 inches (1.310 m) and 3.75 lbs. (1.7 kg), and adult females 3 feet 11 inches (1.2 m) and 2.9 lbs. (1.3 kg) in some southern populations. The largest specimen ever measured was 6 feet 3 inches (1.89 m) in length. Dorsal scale rows at midbody number 23 or 24 (21–26) and are keeled. Males have 158–177 ventral scales and 20–30 subcaudals; corresponding counts in females are 163–183 and 13–26. The scales between the supraoculars are small, numerous, and arranged in 5–8 irregular longitudinal rows.

The ground color varies from yellow to black and may include shades of brown, tan, or gray. The dorsal pattern consists of 15–34

Fig. 19. Timber rattlesnake (*Crotalus horridus*). Photo by Mike Price

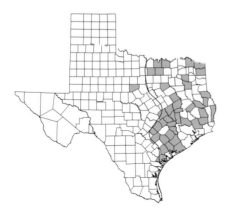

Fig 20. Known occurrences, by county, of the timber rattlesnake (*Crotalus horridus*).

dark transverse chevron or irregularly V-shaped markings. The sooty brown or black coloration of the tail may extend forward on the body some distance and may obscure the posterior transverse bands. Most Texas specimens have a distinct reddish or orange vertebral stripe, 1–4 scales wide, which extends from the neck backward to the tail. The snout and crown of the head may have considerable dark brown or black pigmentation, and a brown stripe 2–3 scales wide may extend from the posterior edge of the eye downward to the angle of the mouth or slightly beyond.

DIFFERENTIATING SIMILAR SPECIES The only other species of rattlesnake native to Texas with an entirely black tail is the blacktailed rattlesnake, but in that species the black coloration is restricted to the tail and does not extend forward onto the body. In addition, the blacktailed rattlesnake lacks a reddish or orange vertebral stripe and transverse dorsal chevron markings. The scales on the crown of the head of the timber rattlesnake are smaller and more numerous than those on the blacktailed rattlesnake. The dorsal processes of the vertebrae of the timber rattlesnake are enlarged compared with those of the blacktailed rattlesnake, giving the former a more pronounced ridged backbone. A hybrid western diamondback crossed with a timber rattlesnake was recently reported from Wise County.

HABITAT Timber rattlesnakes, as the name might suggest, occupy forested areas of central and eastern Texas, such as the Cross Timbers, bottomland hardwoods, and pine woodlands. Most individuals prefer areas with at least 50% coverage by closed canopies and thick ground vegetation, but pregnant females will seek out more open habitats, where they spend considerable time basking, thereby elevating their body temperature and enhancing gestation. Home ranges may be as large as 494 acres (200 hectares) for males. Water is not a barrier; radio-telemetered individuals in Nacogdoches County are known to have crossed the Angelina River.

BEHAVIOR This is a relatively mild-tempered species. Individuals use the ability of their patterning to blend in with the environment as their first line of defense. Males travel greater linear distances than females within their home ranges, especially during the breeding season. At that time, males may move more than a mile a week, and cover areas more than a mile in diameter, in search of females. Extended periods of time may be spent in centers of activity that usually compose less than 10% of an individual's home range. Except for pregnant females, which are rather sedentary, individuals may shift their centers of activity throughout their home ranges as the seasons progress.

REPRODUCTION Little is known about the reproductive habits of this species in Texas. Females in northern populations may not reproduce until they are nine or ten years old, and then produce a litter only once every three or four years. Since the active season in Texas is longer, it can be inferred that females attain sexual maturity at an earlier age and reproduce more frequently. Males and females from Kansas and South Carolina attain sexual maturity at about 3 feet 3 inches (1 m) in length, when females are three (KS) or four (sc) years old, and males (sc) are six years old. Females may reproduce only every second or third year after that. Mating activity in Texas occurs in late summer and continues until snakes move to hibernation areas in the fall. Females presumably store sperm until spring activity resumes. Litter size ranges from 5–16. Young, born in late summer to early fall, range from 11–17 inches (29–43 cm) in length.

PREY AND PREDATORS Timber rattlesnakes are ambush predators, often lying for long periods of time in an S-shaped coil with their heads perpendicular to pathways, such as the long axis of a fallen log, used by small mammals. These snakes eat a wide variety of such prey, including white-footed mice, cotton rats, squirrels, and rabbits. In Texas, other prey include the eastern cottontail, gray squirrel, and fox squirrel. In Louisiana, the northern bobwhite has also been recorded.

Predators of this species in Texas are unknown. The common king snake is known to eat them in Louisiana. Evidence suggests they were occasionally eaten by Native Americans, especially during times of relative food shortage.

VENOM CHARACTERISTICS Venom yields are large in adults, averaging 140 mg (95–150), with a maximum of 300 mg dry weight. The fangs are relatively long (0.35–0.43 inches [9–11 mm] in adults). As with the western diamondback rattlesnake and the western rattlesnake, the potency of the venom appears to be higher in newborns than in adults. Recent research indicates polymorphism in venom types in this species, with venoms characterized as primarily neurotoxic or hemorrhagic, as exhibiting both properties, or as neither. Canebrake toxin, a bipolar molecule with a minimum molecular weight of about 23,000 daltons, greatly enhances the lethality of any venom type. LD_{50} values (ip) from wild-caught specimens possessing primarily neurotoxic venoms with canebrake toxin are 0.22–1.0 mg/kg; for hemorrhagic venoms lacking canebrake toxin, 2.2–8.0 mg/kg; and for venoms possessing both properties, 1.3–1.9 mg/kg. All three venom types may occur in Texas. In another study, an average LD_{50} value (ip) of 0.4 (0.3–0.5) mg/kg was recorded for the most toxic venom type. A corresponding value for the least toxic variety of timber rattlesnake venom is 5.3 (4.0–6.6) mg/kg. Other published lethality values for this species are an LD_{50} of 2.91 mg/kg (ip), 2.63 mg/kg (iv), and 2.25–15.63 mg/kg (sc). The lethal human dose is unknown and undoubtedly variable, but has been estimated at 75–100 mg of venom. This venom exhibits high 5'-nucleotidase and hyaluronidase activities.

FOSSIL RECORD Pleistocene fossils from Harris and Travis counties are the only records of this species in Texas.

REMARKS Southern populations for many years were considered a distinct subspecies, the canebrake rattlesnake (*C. h. atricaudatus*). The weight of current evidence suggests that this is a subjective distinction; there appear to be no geographically coherent genetic or morphological patterns throughout the range of this species that would support this distinction. Rather, it appears the species reinvaded its northern range from southern refugia following the close of the last glacial period in North America, about 10,000 years ago. This may have resulted in a population divergence that warrants taxonomic recognition, but this remains to be determined.

Northern populations, particularly those in New England, are in serious trouble from long-term prosecution and habitat destruction combined with a life-history pattern of late-maturing individuals producing few offspring. The species enjoys some form of protection in most of these states, but the efficacy of these measures remains to be determined. This species is protected in the state of Texas, where it is listed as a threatened species. Natural longevities are unknown, but a captive individual from Texas lived in excess of thirty years.

The name *horridus* (Latin) means "horrible" or "dreadful," a reference to its venomous nature and the reactions to it of the first European colonists to the northeastern United States.

ROCK RATTLESNAKE
Crotalus lepidus (Kennicott, 1861)

CONTENT Five subspecies are recognized. Two occur in the United States, the mottled rock rattlesnake (*C. l. lepidus*) and the banded rock rattlesnake (*C. l. klauberi*), and both can be found in Texas.

Fig. 21. Mottled rock rattlesnake (*Crotalus lepidus lepidus*) from Val Verde County. Photo by Mike Price

Fig. 22. Banded rock rattlesnake (*Crotalus lepidus klauberi*) from Hudspeth County. Photo by Mike Price

DESCRIPTION Rock rattlesnakes are small, relatively slender rattle-snakes, with adult males typically 15–20 inches (38–50 cm) in length, and females somewhat smaller. The largest verifiable record was of an individual 2 feet 9 inches (82.8 cm) in length. Scale rows at midbody number 21–26, and there are 14–24 scales on top of the head between and in front of the eyes. Males have 147–172 ventral and 20–33 subcaudal scales; comparable counts in females are 149–170 and 16–24. The rattle is large and well-developed in proportion to the body. The basic ground color varies considerably with geographic location, and individuals within a population tend to match the background coloration of the rocks in which they live (although individuals are incapable of changing color during their lifetimes). Newborn snakes have yellow tails of varying hue, fading as they age; the head and tail of adults are the same color as the body. These colors include chalky white, buff, tan, pink, red, green, blue gray, and sometimes almost black. Some populations of the banded rock rattlesnake exhibit sexual dichromatism: males are basically green dorsally, and females are gray with more mottling. This phenomenon is unreported in Texas populations. Superimposed upon the ground color is a dorsal pattern of 15–25 narrow, dark brown or black crossbands, without light borders, which start behind the head and extend onto the tail. Individuals of the subspecies *lepidus* have 1–3 indistinct crossbands between each pair of primary bands, giving them a mottled appearance, and possess a dark stripe extending backward from each eye to the corner of the mouth. Individuals of the subspecies *klauberi* (El Paso and Culberson counties) lack the secondary crossbands and the dark stripe from the eye, and have a pair of light-brown to black blotches on the back of the head. There is a broad zone of intergradation between these subspecies in West Texas, within which individuals may possess some combination of these as well as other scale characteristics. The color of the belly varies from white to gray, with small gray or brown blotches or flecks, especially toward the sides and tail. Occasional specimens exhibit aberrant patterns, and patternless individuals have been collected from El Paso and Val Verde counties.

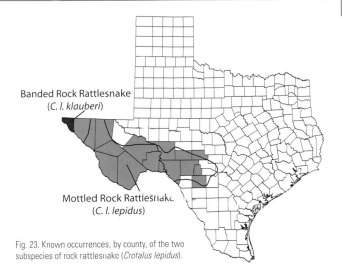

Fig. 23. Known occurrences, by county, of the two subspecies of rock rattlesnake (*Crotalus lepidus*).

DIFFERENTIATING SIMILAR SPECIES The combination of a small size, a vertically divided upper preocular scale, a relatively well-developed rattle, and a distinct color pattern will distinguish this species from others native to Texas.

HABITAT This species is an inhabitant of rough terrain such as rocky canyons, boulder fields, and talus slopes, and can sometimes be found in caves. It occurs at elevations as low as 1,155 feet (350 m) along the Pecos River and Rio Grande valleys, and as high as 8,580 feet (2,600 m) in the Guadalupe Mountains of West Texas. Characteristic vegetation types within their occupied habitats include xeric desert forms (that is, those requiring only a small amount of water) such as acacia, agave, sotol, and yucca; rock rattlesnakes may be found in juniper, pinyon, and oak communities at higher or more sheltered sites. This species may be abundant in a given area, but individuals are seldom seen, because of their behavior. The rock rattlesnake, more than any other species of rattlesnake in Texas, tends to occur as isolated populations, separated from others by unsuitable or unoccupied terrain (see below).

BEHAVIOR These snakes are shy and secretive, well camouflaged, and rarely seen by the casual observer; they will bite readily if disturbed. When active, they frequently hide in cracks and crevices, under rocks or rock ledges, or under vegetation. There are two primary activity periods during the summer: one from about six to 10 in the morning, and another from 6 in the evening to midnight. These periods can be lengthened or shortened by environmental conditions such as rainfall or drought.

REPRODUCTION Extended ritualized combat between males occurs in this species and, as in other viperids, appears to be a contest for social dominance. Litter size is correlated with female body size, and ranges from 2–6 young. Females can reproduce every year if they can eat enough food and sequester sufficient energy reserves. Young are born as early as July.

PREY AND PREDATORS These snakes are ambush predators, often lying motionless in an S-shaped coil while waiting for prey to move within striking distance. The favorite prey are lizards. Small snakes and arthropods such as grasshoppers are occasionally eaten, the latter especially by young individuals. Young snakes use their yellow tails as lures to attract prey within striking distance. Species on the menu in Texas include the hispid cotton rat, kangaroo rat, Texas horned lizard, canyon lizard, crevice spiny lizard, Texas spotted whiptail, Chihuahuan hook-nosed snake, and cliff chirping frog. An incident in which a collared lizard had a snake by the neck and was choking it was reported from El Paso County; although this species of lizard preys upon other reptiles as well, it is impossible to say with certainty whether this was a predatory or defensive bite on the part of the lizard.

The coachwhip and Trans-Pecos copperhead have been reported as predators of this species in Texas.

VENOM CHARACTERISTICS Venom yields from adults are small, ranging from 5 to 25 mg, with a maximum of 33 mg (dry weight), based on limited data. Published LD_{50} ranges are 0.38–5.0 mg/kg (ip), 9.0 mg/kg (iv), and 11.55–23.95 mg/kg (sc). There is considerable variation in venom biochemistry, which appears to be concordant with geographic distribution. The fangs are relatively short (0.12–0.16 inches [3–4 mm] in adults).

DIFFERENTIATING SIMILAR SPECIES The only other species of rattle-snake native to Texas with an entirely black tail is the timber rattlesnake, but in that species the black coloration extends forward on the body for some distance. The blacktailed rattlesnake lacks the vertebral orange stripe and the transverse dorsal bands or chevron markings of the timber rattlesnake. The scales on the crown of the head of the blacktailed rattlesnake are larger and fewer than those on the timber rattlesnake. In addition, the dorsal processes of the vertebrae of the blacktailed rattlesnake are reduced compared with those of the timber rattlesnake, giving it a less-pronounced ridged backbone.

HABITAT This is a species found in rocky, roughland habitats in xeric or semixeric areas throughout its range. It is uncommon on the Edwards Plateau, seemingly confined to narrow, well-vegetated canyons, sinkholes, and similar features. In West Texas, it can be found in all suitable habitats, but is most common from foothills and bajadas with native bunchgrasses, ocotillo, yucca, and acacia at about 4,100 feet (1,240 m), through pine-oak woodlands at about 8,500 feet (2,576 m). Throughout its range, it can be found in caves and crevices, where individuals undoubtedly hibernate.

BEHAVIOR This may be the most docile species of the genus in Texas; individuals rarely rattle unless directly disturbed, but rather depend on their striking color and pattern characteristics, which provide superb camouflage within the roughland habitats they occupy. Individuals may travel as much as 13.6 miles (22 km) during an activity season, and may have home ranges as large as 15 acres (6 hectares). Blacktails may be active all year long and at temperatures as low as 50°F (10°C), although most activity takes place from March through October at body temperatures of about 86°F (30°C).

REPRODUCTION Very little is known about this species. Males may accompany females for several weeks in the field during the summer. Mating occurs in late summer or early fall, which is also the time when male-male combat most frequently occurs. Females store sperm until their spring emergence; ovulation and fertilization take place at this time. The young are born in July or August in litters of 8–10, at a size of 9–11 inches (23–28 cm). Females may give birth in communal rookeries, and remain with the young for a period of time after birth.

PREY AND PREDATORS Although data are few, newborn and young blacktails probably prey upon small mammals such as shrews, pocket mice, and white-footed mice, as well as lizard species such as the canyon spiny lizard, the crevice spiny lizard, and the tree lizard, which are abundant within their occupied habitat. Adult snakes eat larger mammals, such as rabbits, squirrels, wood rats, kangaroo rats, and occasionally ground-nesting birds or those that nest low to the ground. The largest of these prey items may provide an individual snake up to one-third of its basic metabolic requirements for an activity season. Like other rattlesnakes, blacktails seek out places where they can bask after eating, thereby raising their body temperatures as much as 9°F (5°C) higher than in the nonfeeding condition and aiding digestion. On the menu in Texas are the pallid bat, white-ankled mouse, and the crevice spiny lizard. In neighboring Chihuahua, Mexico, the cactus mouse, deer mouse, white-throated wood rat, rock pocket mouse, silky pocket mouse, and Merriam's kangaroo rat are known to be prey.

Predators in Texas include the red-tailed hawk and common king snake. Evidence suggests that blacktailed rattlesnakes were occasionally eaten by Native Americans, especially during times of relative food shortage.

VENOM CHARACTERISTICS Venom yields from adults are moderate, based on very limited data, averaging 180–286 mg (dry weight), with a maximum of 540 mg. As with other species, there are significant individual and age-related differences in venom properties, which have important biomedical implications. An LD_{50} range of 2.7–7.0 mg/kg (ip) has been reported. The venom has strong anticoagulant and high protease activities. The fangs are relatively long (0.39–0.55 inches [10–14 mm] in adults).

FOSSIL RECORD Pleistocene fossils have been found in Val Verde County.

REMARKS Natural life spans are unknown, but a captive adult from Texas lived in excess of twenty years. The name *molossus* (Latin) refers to the Molossian hound of antiquity; the etymology is obscure, but may be due to an old and little-used common name for this species, the dog-faced rattlesnake.

MOJAVE RATTLESNAKE
Crotalus scutulatus (Kennicott, 1861)

CONTENT Two subspecies are recognized; the Mojave rattlesnake (*C. s. scutulatus*) occurs in Texas.

DESCRIPTION Mojaves are medium-sized, somewhat slender rattlesnakes, with adults ranging between 2–3 feet (60–90 cm) in length. Maximum recorded size is 4 feet 6 inches (1.37 m), for a male from Brewster County. Scale rows at midbody number 21–29, and there are 8–23 scales on top of the head from the nose to between and in front of the eyes. The scales between the supraoculars in the Mojave rattlesnake are relatively large and lie in only 2–3 rows. Males have 165–190 ventral and 21–29 subcaudal scales; comparable counts in females are 167–192 and 15–25.

The dorsal ground color can be various shades or combinations of green, yellow, olive, gray, or brown. A wide, poorly defined dark stripe extends from each eye downward and backward to the angle of the mouth; a well-defined light stripe borders the dark one posteriorly and extends backward above the angle of the mouth. The dorsal pattern consists of 24–36 dark gray to brown blotches, usually diamond-shaped but occasionally oval to hexagonal, each with a one-scale-wide border of uniformly light-colored scales. The tail is distinctly banded with black and white rings, the white ones as much as three times as wide as the black. The lower half of the basal rattle segment is usually much lighter in color than the remainder of the rattle.

DIFFERENTIATING SIMILAR SPECIES The only other species native to Texas with a distinctively black-and-white banded tail is the western diamondback rattlesnake. The latter species has smaller scales on the top of the head (rarely 3, and usually 4 or more intersupraoculars), the light postocular stripe extends downward before or at the angle of the mouth, the black and white tail bands

Fig. 26. Mojave rattlesnake (*Crotalus scutulatus scutulatus*). Photo by Mike Price

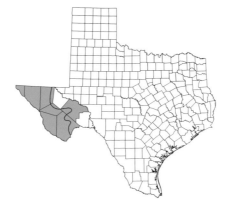

Fig. 27. Known occurrences, by county, of the Mojave rattlesnake (*Crotalus scutulatus scutulatus*).

are approximately equal in width, the scales bordering each dorsal blotch are multicolored (making the pattern less distinctive), and the last half of the basal rattle segment is unicolored. Hybridization between the two species does occur in the Big Bend, and hybrid individuals may exhibit one or more characteristics that are intermediate between the two.

Fig. 28. Rattlesnake patterning.

A. Mojave rattlesnake.

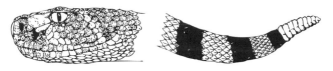

B. Western diamondback rattlesnake.

HABITAT This species occurs in open creosote-bush desert flats and desert grasslands, generally without rocky soils, at elevations below 5,000 feet (1,515 m).

BEHAVIOR This species is almost always nocturnal during the summer months, but can be found during the day at other times during its activity season, which extends from March through October. It has a reputation for being highly aggressive, which, combined with the increased toxicity of its venom, would place this species at the high end of the danger scale. Fortunately, this reputation is overstated: individuals are just as likely to attempt to escape as they are to assume the characteristic defensive posture of congeners such as the western diamondback rattlesnake. Individuals hibernate singly or in small groups, and may be active at the mouth of hibernacula on warm days.

REPRODUCTION Very little is known about reproduction in this species. Mating may take place at any time during the summer activity season. Females inseminated late during the season may store sperm for use in fertilizing ova after their spring emergence from hibernation. Young are born from July through September, with a peak in August. Litter size averages about 9, with a range of 5–13. A natural hybrid with *Crotalus viridis* from Hudspeth County has been reported.

PREY AND PREDATORS Although juveniles may take a wide variety of prey, from insects to small mammals, adults eat primarily mammals. In Texas, the Texas banded gecko, spiny lizards, and western whiptail are known to be eaten. In neighboring Chihuahua, Mexico, the black-tailed jackrabbit, desert cottontail, cactus mouse, deer mouse, Merriam's kangaroo rat, bannertail kangaroo rat, rock pocket mouse, desert pocket mouse, silky pocket mouse, and spotted ground squirrel are on the menu.

VENOM CHARACTERISTICS Venom yields from adults are moderate, based on very limited data, averaging 180–286 mg (dry weight), with a maximum of 540 mg dry weight. There are distinct biochemical and toxicological differences in venoms from different populations throughout the geographic range of this species. The Texas population has the more toxic venom, although this can vary even within the offspring of a single litter. These populations exhibit considerable neurotoxic activity in their venom, with little local edema or tissue damage but significant systemic effects resulting from bites. An average LD_{50} (ip) of 0.24 mg/kg (0.13–0.54) has been reported for the most toxic venom variety. Comparable values for a less toxic venom variant are 3.0 mg/kg (2.3–3.8). Additional LD_{50} values reported are 0.12–0.21 mg/kg (iv) and 0.31 mg/kg (sc). The lethal human dose is unknown and undoubtedly variable, but has been estimated at 10–15 mg. This is generally recognized as one of the most dangerous species of rattlesnakes in North America because of its relatively large size, the irritable tendency of certain individuals, and the potency of the venom. The venom is devoid of hemorrhagic and high alkaline phosphomonoesterase activities.

The fangs are relatively long (0.39–0.55 inches [10–14 mm]) in adults.

FOSSIL RECORD No fossils of this species are known to occur in Texas.

REMARKS Natural longevities are unknown for this species. A captive individual exhibited a known age of fourteen years and was still alive at the time of the survey. The name *scutulatus* (Latin) means "diamond- or lozenge-shaped" and refers to the dorsal color pattern.

WESTERN RATTLESNAKE
Crotalus viridis (Rafinesque, 1818)

CONTENT Three subspecies are recognized. The prairie rattlesnake (*C. v. viridis*) occurs in Texas.

DESCRIPTION Prairie rattlesnakes are medium-sized, relatively slender rattlesnakes, with adults ranging from 2 feet 8 inches to 3 feet 10 inches (81.2–116.8 cm) in total length. The largest recorded specimen was 4 feet 11.75 inches (1.51 m) in total length. Scale rows at midbody number 27 (23–29) and are keeled. Males have 164–189 ventral and 21–31 subcaudal scales; the corresponding counts in females are 170–196 and 14–26. There are 4 internasal scales in contact with the rostral scale.

The ground color is usually tan or light brown, but can be greenish gray, olive green, or greenish brown. The dorsal pattern consists of 33–57 squarish, dark brown blotches with narrow but distinct white borders; toward the tail, the blotches tend to become less distinct, forming crossbands, and the white borders tend to disappear. The tail is banded but not in black-and-white; there are 6–15 brown bands in males and 4–11 in females. Up to three series of indistinct lateral body blotches may occur. Two

Fig. 29. Prairie rattlesnake (*Crotalus viridis viridis*). Photo by Mike Price

white flash marks occur on each side of the face: one extends from in front of the eye downward to the line of the mouth, and the other extends from behind the eye backward above the angle of the jaw. An albino from Lipscomb County has been reported.

DIFFERENTIATING SIMILAR SPECIES The western diamondback rattlesnake and the Mojave rattlesnake both have distinct black-and-white banded tails, dorsal patterns that are diamond-shaped rather than square-shaped (on at least the front part of the body), and only two rather than four internasal scales touching the rostral. The massasauga has nine large plates rather than many small scales covering the crown of the head.

HABITAT A general and ubiquitous inhabitant of grasslands throughout its range, it can characteristically be found associated with ground squirrel and prairie dog colonies within the High Plains, Rolling Plains, and Trans-Pecos natural regions of Texas, where it uses these animals for food and their burrows for shelter. It is less commonly encountered within escarpment breaks, floodplains, and desert scrub habitats, which are more frequently occupied by congeners such as the western diamondback rattlesnake.

BEHAVIOR Both male and nonpregnant female snakes leave winter den sites in the spring, and may travel 4.3 miles (7 km) or more until they reach areas of relatively high prey densities, where individual snakes may remain for the first half of the summer. Females continue to search out prey patches after that, whereas males begin to spend their time searching for females with which to mate. Snakes seek out winter dens when body temperatures fall below about 84°F (29°C), often returning to the same one year after year. Individuals may remain active in the den throughout the winter, including basking at its entrance on warm days, as long as body temperatures can be maintained at about 52°F (11°C).

REPRODUCTION Little is known about the reproductive habits of this species in Texas. Elsewhere, mating takes place from late summer into fall, and mated females store sperm throughout the winter. Males are active during the spring while replenishing energy reserves, and warm body temperatures are required to initiate the annual sperm-production cycle. Pregnant females leave the winter den in the spring and travel short distances to specific

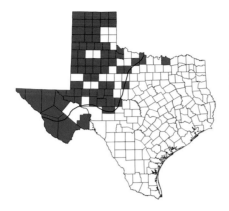

Fig. 30. Known occurrences, by county, of the prairie rattlesnake (*Crotalus viridis viridis*).

areas called rookeries. Here they remain relatively sedentary, feed little, maintain elevated body temperatures to aid gestation, and give birth in the late summer or early fall. Several dozen females may congregate in the same rookery. Litter size is correlated with female body size, averages about 9 young, and ranges from 5–14. Newborns are able to follow the scent trails of adults to find overwintering den sites. A natural hybrid with *Crotalus scutulatus* from Hudspeth County has been reported.

PREY AND PREDATORS Tongue-flicking rates are greatly enhanced after snakes strike prey objects. Through this behavior, a snake uses chemical cues to find envenomated prey, which may have traveled some distance before death. In Texas, the yellow-faced pocket gopher (scavenged from beneath a hawk's nest), black-tailed prairie dog, horned lizards, and the common side-blotched lizard have been recorded in the diet.

No predators have been noted in Texas.

VENOM CHARACTERISTICS Venom yields from adults are moderate, averaging 44 mg (25–100), with a maximum of 165 mg dry weight. Additional reported LD_{50} values are 1.1–1.61 mg/kg (iv), 1.25–2.3 mg/kg (ip), and 5.5–14.8 mg/kg (sc). As with the western diamondback rattlesnake and the timber rattlesnake, the potency of the venom appears to be higher in newborns than in adults. As with other species of rattlesnakes, some venom components vary with geographic location. The fangs are of moderate length (0.28–0.35 inches [7–9 mm] in adults).

FOSSIL RECORD Recent/Archaic fossils of this species in Texas have been found in El Paso, Oldham, and Terrell counties.

REMARKS Natural longevities are unknown; a captive individual lived in excess of nineteen years. There is some suggestion that gopher snakes mimic this species to some degree, since elsewhere where their ranges overlap, they share aspects of color, pattern, and behavior. The precise nature of this relationship, if any, in Texas remains to be studied. The name *viridis* (Latin) means "green," in reference to a typical ground color in this species.

MASSASAUGA

Sistrurus catenatus (Rafinesque, 1818)

CONTENT Three subspecies are recognized; the desert massasauga (*S. c. edwardsii*) and the western massasauga (*S. c. tergeminus*) occur in Texas.

DESCRIPTION Massasaugas are small rattlesnakes, with adults typically 18–26 inches (45–65 cm) in length. The largest recorded specimens are 35 inches (88 cm) for *tergeminus* and 21 inches (53 cm) for *edwardsii*. There are 21–27 (usually 23 or 25) scale rows at midbody, all but 1 or 2 keeled. Males possess between 129–155 ventral and 24–36 subcaudal scales; corresponding ranges in females are 132–160 and 19–29. Up to 9 distal subcaudals may be divided. The top of the head bears the nine enlarged plates characteristic of the genus.

This is a light gray to grayish brown snake with 27–50 grayish brown middorsal blotches, which are bordered with dark brown or black and narrowly outlined with white. Two or three lateral series of similar but smaller blotches occur on each side. The lateral and middorsal blotches are rarely in contact; the lowermost lateral series may extend onto the ventral scales, which range from heavily spotted with dark pigment to immaculate. Brown crossbands on the tail number 3–11. A transverse brown bar crosses the head in front of the eyes. A variable dark brown marking, often lyre-shaped, extends backward on top of the head. A white-edged dark

Fig. 31. Desert massasauga (*Sistrurus catenatus edwardsii*). Photo by Mike Price

Fig. 32. Western massasauga (*Sistrurus catenatus tergeminus*). Photo by Tom Sinclair

brown stripe, 2–3 scales wide, extends backward to the angle of the mouth and beyond; this white edge extends forward on the face to the pit organ. The tail is short and the rattle small. Newborn young have yellow tails, which assume typical coloration within a year.

DIFFERENTIATING SIMILAR SPECIES The pygmy rattlesnake is smaller and lighter in color and has a middorsal light orange or orange-brown stripe; its upper preocular scales are separated from the postnasal scale by a large loreal scale. All other species of rattle-snakes native to Texas have many smaller scales, rather than 9 large plates, on top of the head. Hognose snakes (genus *Heterodon*), which are nonvenomous, lack any semblance of a rattle or the facial pit characteristic of rattlesnakes, and have a distinctly upturned rostral scale.

HABITAT This is a characteristic inhabitant of tall-grass prairies in Central Texas, such as the Grand Prairie southwest of Fort Worth and at Waco, as well as short-grass prairies and open thorn scrub elsewhere in the state. Seasonal wetlands are often important features of the occupied habitat. Massasaugas tend to hibernate in wetter areas, and move to drier or upland habitats during the summer.

BEHAVIOR This species is nocturnal or crepuscular (active at dusk) during the hot summer months, but diurnal during spring and fall. It can be found from March through October, and is most

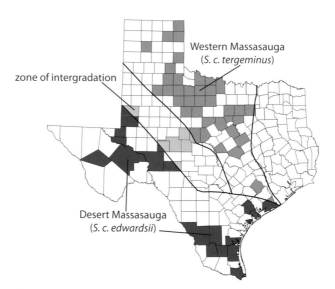

Fig. 33. Known occurrences, by county, of the two subspecies of the massasauga (*Sistrurus catenatus*).

active from April to early June in north-central Texas and from July to August in the Panhandle. This may reflect the tendency of individual snakes to move farther and more often during the summer than at other times during the activity season. This species may be abundant in a given area, but individuals, which are cryptic, may seldom be seen. Massasaugas are good swimmers and readily enter the water. They are relatively sedentary snakes, moving on average about 33 feet (10 m) a day and occupying a home range of less than 11,960 square yards (10,000 m²). Gravid females occupy smaller areas than other adults.

REPRODUCTION Little is known concerning Texas populations. Courtship behavior resembles that seen in the western diamond-back rattlesnake, although it is not as prolonged. Females attain sexual maturity at about 15.75 inches (40 cm) in length, perhaps in their third year of life. Litter size ranges from 3–11. Individual females may exhibit parental care, remaining with newborns until their first shed.

PREY AND PREDATORS Massasaugas are opportunistic predators and take a wide variety of vertebrate and invertebrate prey. Known food items in Texas include the short-tailed shrew, southern short-tailed shrew, least shrew, desert shrew, cinereus shrew, northern pygmy mouse, plains pocket mouse, hispid pocket mouse, Merriam's pocket mouse, grasshopper mouse, northern grasshopper mouse, white-footed mouse, deer mouse, western harvest mouse, plains harvest mouse, meadow jumping mouse, woodland jumping mouse, prairie vole, northern bobwhite and lark sparrow eggs, red-winged blackbird fledglings, field sparrow, eastern collared lizard, lesser earless lizard, Texas horned lizard, Texas spiny lizard, eastern fence lizard, tree lizard, side-blotched lizard, Great Plains skink, ground skink, Texas spotted whiptail , six-lined racerunner, desert grassland whiptail, smooth green snake, ground snake, DeKay's brown snake, plains black-headed snake, garter snake, common garter snake, lined snake, massasauga, spring peeper, plains spadefoot, leopard frog, Rio Grande leopard frog, giant desert centipede, and crickets. Greene and Oliver (1965) reported an individual attempting to swallow a freshly killed western hognose snake.

Weasels and their kin, feral hogs, roadrunners, Swainson's hawks, northern harriers, loggerhead shrikes, eastern racers, and bullfrogs include massasaugas in their diets. There is an interesting report of a raccoon consuming a massasauga in McCulloch County, Texas; massasaugas are not known from this county, but are common in the adjacent one to the west.

VENOM CHARACTERISTICS Venom yields from adults are small, averaging 14 mg (dry weight) with a maximum of 37 mg. LD_{50} ranges of 0.2–0.9 mg/kg (ip) and 5.25–6.8 mg/kg (sc) have been reported. The lethal human dose is unknown and undoubtedly variable, but has been estimated at 30–40 mg; human fatalities from this species are rare, and none have been reported in Texas. The fangs are relatively short (0.16–0.24 inches [4–6 mm] in adults).

FOSSIL RECORD There is a remarkable record of a Pliocene fossil for this species in Scurry County.

REMARKS Modification or destruction of its native grassland habitats may be eliminating this species from areas throughout its range, although such long-term, widespread trends are hard to pin down with accurate data. The species is certainly becoming less abundant in many areas.

John K. Strecker considered this species to be "on the road to extinction" in the Texas Panhandle as early as 1910 because of the widespread conversion of habitat to agricultural purposes. Gently rolling tall-grass prairies west and south of Fort Worth, where the massasauga was one of the commonest snakes encountered, are now full of subdivisions. According to Strecker, in 1915 massa-saugas were "formerly abundant in the Panhandle district, but farmers report that it is getting scarcer every year. Mr. Lutrell of Claude, Armstrong County, informs me that he has often killed from fifty to sixty during one wheat season, but that during the past four or five years he has not seen more than half a dozen in any one year."

Natural longevities are unknown; captive individuals have lived in excess of twelve years (*S. c. edwardsii*) and twenty years (*S. c. tergeminus*).

The name *catenatus* (Latin) means "chained" or "chain-like" and refers to the dorsal pattern. The name *tergeminus* (Latin) means "threefold" or "triple" and refers to the three rows of prominent dorsolateral blotches in this form. The name *edwardsii* is a patronym honoring L. A. Edwards, a U.S. Army surgeon who collected the type-specimen on one of the mid-nineteenth-century government-sponsored exploration expeditions in the American West. Incidentally, the common name for this species means "great river-mouth" in the Chippewa language, probably in reference to the marshy habitat of this snake in the region of the Great Lakes.

PYGMY RATTLESNAKE
Sistrurus miliarius (Linnaeus, 1766)

CONTENT Three subspecies are recognized; the western pygmy rattlesnake (*S. m. streckeri*) occurs in Texas.

DESCRIPTION Pygmies, as their name implies, are small rattlesnakes, with adults reaching 1–1.5 feet (30–50 cm) in length. The largest recorded specimen was a male 25 inches (63.8 cm) in length, although the specimen was in captivity, so growth was probably artificially enhanced. The tail is slender and the rattle tiny. Dorsal scale rows, all keeled, number 21 (occasionally 23) at midbody. Ventral scales number 123–135 and average 127 in males and 129 in females. Subcaudals number 27–38 in males and 27–34 in females, the distal 1–11 often divided. There are 9 large plates, characteristic of the genus, on top of the head. The relatively large loreal scale is in broad contact with the prefrontal scale and separates the preocular scales from the postnasal ones.

The dorsal ground color is pale grayish brown, with a light stippling of darker brown. A median dorsal series of 23–42 dark brown blotches, conspicuously wider than they are long and irregularly bordered with white, extend from the neck to the tail. An additional one or two lateral series of blotches may occur on each side. A number of irregular brown blotches occur on the snout, and a wide lightly colored bar crosses the head behind

71

Fig. 34. Western pygmy rattlesnake (*Sistrurus miliarius streckeri*). Photo by Tom Sinclair

them. A pair of undulating brown stripes, sometimes forming a lyre-shaped pattern, extend from the bar to the neck. A dark brown cheek stripe extends posteriorly from each eye to the angle of the mouth. A reddish brown middorsal stripe extends from the back of the head to the base of the tail. More or less transverse dorsal bands, 7–14 in number, occur on the tail itself. The tails of newborns are sulfur yellow in color, fading with age.

DIFFERENTIATING SIMILAR SPECIES Massasaugas are larger and darker, and the upper preocular scales are in contact with the postnasal scale. All other species of rattlesnakes native to Texas have many smaller scales, rather than 9 large plates, on top of the head. Hognose snakes (genus *Heterodon*), which are nonvenomous, lack any semblance of a rattle or the facial pit characteristic of rattlesnakes, and have a distinctly upturned rostral scale.

HABITAT Individuals are frequently found beneath decaying logs, pieces of bark, palmetto fronds, and other organic debris in open upland loblolly pine–hardwood forests, bottomland hardwoods, mesic grasslands of eastern Texas, and the open agricultural lands, rice fields, and bar ditches along the upper Coastal Plain.

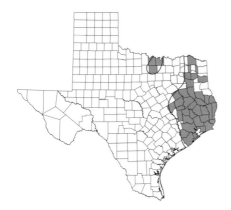

Fig. 35. Known occurrences, by county, of the western pygmy rattlesnake (*Sistrurus miliarius streckeri*).

BEHAVIOR Very little is known about the behavior of this species in the wild. It is probably an ambush predator, since individuals are highly cryptic and spend most of their time hidden. The sound of the tiny rattle is barely audible and easily mistaken for the buzzing of a cicada or some other insect. When disturbed, these snakes may bob their heads vertically in addition to rattling. Individuals may be surface active throughout the year at body temperatures of 59–99°F (15–37°C), particularly when water-table levels are high.

REPRODUCTION Pygmy rattlesnakes in Texas, like their Florida counterparts, probably mate in the fall. Females are gravid in the spring and give birth in July and August. Most females in the Florida population studied were not gravid in consecutive years. Average litter size is about 6, with a normal range of 2–11 young. Larger females give birth to larger litters; one large female produced a litter of 32 young. Newborn snakes weigh 0.07–0.21 ounces (2–6 gm) and are about 4–8 inches (11–20 cm) in total length. Females may remain with newborns until they shed their skins for the first time. Males engage is physical combat (the so-called "combat dance") to establish social dominance, which probably facilitates access to females. Male combat rituals are subdued.

PREY AND PREDATORS A variety of prey are taken, including insects, centipedes, frogs and toads, lizards, small snakes, nestling birds, and small mammals. Juvenile and young snakes may use their brightly colored tail tips to lure prey within striking distance.

The northern cricket frog occurs in the diet of this species in Texas. In Louisiana, green frogs, southern leopard frogs, and crickets are also eaten. In Arkansas, the four-toed salamander, eastern fence lizard, common five-lined skink, little brown skink, and ring-necked snake are known to be taken.

Predators of pygmy rattlesnakes are unknown in Texas.

VENOM CHARACTERISTICS Data are very limited, and exist only for the eastern subspecies. Venom yields from adults are small, ranging from 18–34 mg (dry weight). LD_{50} ranges of 2.8–12.6 mg/kg (iv), 6.0–7.0 mg/kg (ip), and 24.25 mg/kg (sc) have been reported. The fangs are relatively short (0.2–0.24 inches [5–6 mm] in adults). This species is not believed to be capable of inflicting a fatal bite on a person because of its small size and weak venom, and no fatalities are known from the bite of this species.

FOSSIL RECORD No fossils of this species have been recorded in Texas.

REMARKS The natural longevity of this subspecies is unknown, although a captive individual lived in excess of sixteen years. The name *miliarius* (Latin) means "millet" or "millet-like," presumably in reference to the blotched dorsal pattern. The Texas subspecies is named in honor of John K. Strecker of Baylor University, Texas's pioneering herpetologist in the early twentieth century.

ELAPIDAE

This is a relatively recent family of venomous snakes, appearing abruptly in the fossil record of the Old World about 25 million years ago, during the Miocene Epoch. Members apparently dispersed into North America across the Bering land bridge shortly thereafter. Today there are more than 270 species distributed among 62 genera worldwide, with centers of diversity in Africa, Southeast Asia, and Australia. The group includes such familiar kinds as cobras, kraits, mambas, tiger snakes, and coral snakes. Most species lay eggs, but some give birth to live young. All are characterized by having a relatively short and permanently erect fang on each maxilla at the front of the mouth (proteroglyphy). There are replacement fangs located behind the functional one to replace it when necessary. Elapids lack the lever-and-pulley fang mechanism of vipers and pit vipers, and their fangs fit into grooved slots in the floor of the mouth when the mouth is closed.

In coral snakes, a venom gland is located on each side of the upper jaw behind the eye, and is connected by a duct to an open sinus at the base of each fang. The duct is surrounded by a simple mucus gland into which many tiny tubules empty, and the entire system is covered by a tough connective tissue capsule protecting it from injury. Venom is forced from the gland by the contraction of muscles located above and behind it, and is delivered from the fang sinus into the wound by means of the chewing motions characteristic of coral snakes. Small quantities of venom are also secreted from infralabial glands located in the lower jaw.

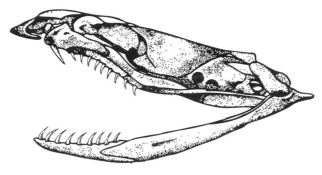

Fig. 36. Side view of the skull of a coral snake, showing one of the two short, fixed fangs at the front of the upper jaw. Note the smaller teeth, which almost always contribute to the bite pattern.

HARLEQUIN CORAL SNAKE
Micrurus fulvius (Linnaeus, 1766)

CONTENT Six subspecies are recognized; the Texas coral snake (*M. f. tener*) occurs in Texas.

DESCRIPTION Texas coral snakes are slender, medium-sized snakes with heads not discernibly larger than their bodies. Adults are typically 15–25 inches (38–63.5 cm) in length; the largest recorded specimen for this subspecies was 3-feet-11.75 inches (1.21 m) in total length, and was found in Brazoria County, Texas. On average, females are larger than males. Scale rows number 15 at midbody and are smooth. The anal plate is divided. Ventral and subcaudal scales number 200–211 and 38–46 in males, and

Fig. 37. Texas coral snake (*Micrurus fulvius tener*). Photo by Mike Price

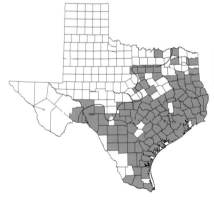

Fig. 38. Known occurrences, by county, of the Texas coral snake (*Micrurus fulvius tener*).

219–227 and 26–34 in females. The nose is black, and there are 10–14 (males) or 15 (females) black body bands. The red body bands are often speckled with irregular black dots, which have a tendency to be concentrated toward the scale tips. The yellow bands are immaculate and 1–2 scales wide. The color bands continue onto the ventral surface. A melanistic individual was collected in Victoria County in 1938, having inflicted a bite after being mistakenly picked up. An albino has been found in Houston, and an aberrant individual with a reduced number of dorsal black rings, several of which were reduced to dorsal blotches, and in which the ventral coloration was almost a solid coral red color, has been reported.

DIFFERENTIATING SIMILAR SPECIES The old adage "red touch yellow, kill a fellow; red touch black, venom lack" still serves to distinguish this species from other brightly banded species of snakes in Texas, all of which are harmless. None of these other species, such as milk snakes (*Lampropeltis triangulum*) and scarlet snakes (*Cemophora coccinea*), have red and yellow (or whitish) bands touching each other. This adage does not work in the New World tropics, however, where the greatest diversity of coral snake species and their mimics occur.

HABITAT This species can be very abundant but never seen because of its secretive and fossorial (underground) habits. A wide variety of terrestrial environments are inhabited, from urban and suburban ones to East Texas pine forests to oak-juniper canyons along the Pecos River, as long as sufficient rock-crevice cover or thick plant litter exists. Coral snakes are found in Central Texas in heavily vegetated mesic lowlands that feature an abundance of

Fig. 39. The Louisiana Milk Snake (*Lampropeltis triangulum amaura*) is one of four coral-snake pretenders in Texas. Photo by Tom Sinclair

organic debris, and on the Edwards Plateau in semiopen valleys and oak-juniper uplands. In south-central Texas, typical habitats include post oak–blackjack oak vegetative communities that include yaupon, Texas bluebonnet, little bluestem, Bermuda grass, and needle grass as common components. Wooded floodplains with dwarf palmettos, pecans, cedar elms, water oaks, black willows, lianas, and Spanish moss are also inhabited. Peat bogs with sphagnum, broadleaf cattail, yaupon, holly, wax myrtle, Mexican plum, and black willows are also inhabited.

BEHAVIOR Coral snakes spend most of their time underground (fossoriality) or sheltering under suitable objects, but can be active on the surface during the day in early spring or at other times when rainfall has saturated the ground. They appear not to be generally surface active at night. Males are most active in the late fall or early spring, when they search for mates, and females are most active in late summer and throughout the fall, when they search for the prey that will allow them to build energy reserves for the next season's reproductive effort. Coral snakes will attempt to escape if discovered, and individuals may engage in complex defensive behavior if prevented from doing so. This includes hiding the head beneath the body coils, mimicking the head with the tail (for example, crawling backward and striking with the tail), erratic body movements, and death feigning. Other individuals can be touchy, and will readily bite if restrained in any way.

REPRODUCTION Males attain sexual maturity at an age of 12–21 months and a length of about 16 inches (40 cm), and females do so at 15 months of age and about 20 inches (50 cm) in length. Mating takes place from October through May, and a clutch of 2–13 eggs is laid in May or June. Clutches of 3, 9, 9, and 7 eggs, laid in June and July, have been reported from Texas specimens. Common nesting sites include inside rotten logs, under rocks, and underground. Eggs hatch from the end of August into October, and hatchlings are about 8 inches (20 cm) long.

PREY AND PREDATORS Coral snakes eat other snakes (ophiophagy), including occasionally each other, as well as elongate lizards such as skinks and glass lizards. Snakes eaten are primarily fossorial or semifossorial. Coral snakes are active foragers, on the move in search of prey, which they may recognize through chemical or visual cues. Prey are grasped and held while chewing movements are employed to work venom into the victim, which is quickly immobilized and usually swallowed headfirst. The eastern fence lizard, common five-lined skink, broad-headed skink, four-lined skink, little brown skink, Texas spotted whiptail, glossy snake, Texas rat snake, yellow-bellied king snake, common king snake, coachwhip, diamondback water snake, rough green snake, eastern patch-nosed snake, ground snake, DeKay's brown snake, flat-headed snake, Smith's black-headed snake, black-necked garter snake, checkered garter snake, western ribbon snake, lined snake, rough earth snake, smooth earth snake, copperhead, and harlequin coral snake are known to be eaten in Texas.

Coral snakes fall prey to a variety of predators, but only bullfrogs in Texas and the common king snake in Louisiana have been documented in the region.

VENOM CHARACTERISTICS Coral snake venom is a complex array of proteins, mostly enzymes and other polypeptides along with nonprotein substances such as riboflavin and metallic salts (zinc, calcium, magnesium, potassium), which act synergistically to produce lethal effects. Coral snake venom produces very little local tissue damage, hemorrhaging, or swelling. Lethal effects from Texas coral snake venom may occur in two ways: venom blocks the junctions between, and interferes with chemical communication between, nerves and muscles, causing death by suffocation when muscles of the respiratory system are paralyzed; venom acts directly on the heart and the cardiovascular system, causing a marked decrease in heart rate, loss of blood pressure, and death from shock. The venom yield for this subspecies is 2–28 mg dry weight, and is positively correlated with body size. Published LD_{50} values include 0.97 mg/kg (ip), 0.28 mg/kg (iv), and 2.60 mg/kg (sc). The lethal human dose is unknown and undoubtedly variable, but has been estimated at 4–7 mg/kg. Coral snakes apparently possess no immunity to their own venom.

Human envenomations are uncommon (less than 40% of reported bites), partly because of the primitive delivery mechanism, small size, and generally inoffensive nature of the snakes. In a definitive study of coral snake bites published in 1987, 34 of 39 patients (87%) were bitten on a finger or thumb, or on the thin skin fold between the finger and thumb. Of the 32 people for whom information was available, only 8 victims suffered "legitimate" bites. Twenty-three others were deliberately handling the snake (14 through misidentification), and 8 of these were inebriated. Human fatalities are now entirely preventable with antivenom treatment coupled with appropriate surgical intervention (see the Snakebite section).

FOSSIL RECORD Pleistocene fossils have been found in Foard, Kendall, and Travis counties.

REMARKS A debate between scientists has existed for over a century about whether the bright coloration of coral snakes is aposematic (serves to warn potential predators of their deadly nature), and, therefore, whether similarly colored nonpoisonous species of snakes derive enhanced protection from potential predators by mimicking the pattern and behavior of coral snakes. The correlative evidence suggests strongly that such is the case, supported by experimental evidence with potential avian predators. However, recent experiments with mammals have produced contrary results, suggesting that more work needs to be done to understand this phenomenon. The ringed pattern of coral snakes may also be disruptive in their natural habitats, serving to conceal and break up the body outline and thus make it more difficult for potential predators to aim an effective attack.

Natural longevities for this species are unknown, but a captive individual lived in excess of eighteen years. This record is a notable accomplishment in itself, since this species is very difficult to maintain in captivity. The name *fulvius* (Latin) means "orange" or "orange yellow," apparently in reference to the faded red bands on the first preserved specimen(s) seen by Linnaeus. The name *tener* (Latin) means "tender" or "delicate" and refers to the slender body style of this form. This snake is considered a full species, *Micrurus tener*, by some authorities.

A WORD ABOUT CONSERVATION

I suspect that many readers of this book are to some extent aware of and can appreciate the oddly paradoxical position, when it comes to the subject of rattlesnakes, of a former herpetologist who worked for a state natural-resource-management agency in Texas. Setting aside the public health aspects and the various prejudices surrounding snakes in general and venomous ones in particular, the controversial flashpoints are the nature of rattlesnake roundups and, more broadly, the commercial exploitation of nongame wildlife. The viewpoint I bring to this area should be evident from reading this book, but let me be clear. I have devoted most of my adult working life (and some of my free time) to the science of herpetology, and a good portion of that to rattlesnakes. I have encountered over a thousand rattlesnakes during the course of my fieldwork, and I have collected many specimens for scientific purposes. I have been on rattlesnake hunts in which gasoline mist was sprayed into dens to flush the snakes out, and I can say that it is a very effective technique. I have eaten rattlesnake meat on field trips, and I can say unequivocally that I prefer chicken. I have always thought that the various parts of a rattlesnake work better when they are on the live animal than they would if wound around my head or waist or holding papers down on my desk. I wrote a letter many years ago to the Muscular Dystrophy Association on behalf of my father, one of the longest-lived patients with muscular dystrophy, objecting to their involvement with rattlesnake roundups on ethical and educational grounds.

Does this mean I am prepared to recommend the abolition of rattlesnake roundups, for example, as a matter of public policy or scientific principle? No. To do so would, in my view, be to attempt to legislate morality or institutionalize ethics, a slippery slope upon which I am unwilling to tread. All I can do in this regard is to argue to the best of my ability for the natural place of rattlesnakes, as a product of the evolutionary process, in the web of life on this planet. I believe that people holding widely diverse viewpoints can understand and appreciate rattlesnakes. My responsibility as a scientist, however, is to safeguard the resource and advance the mission of wildlife management agencies by asking the appropriate questions, examining the data, and coming to the required conclusions. So what do we know about rattlesnakes in Texas?

The use of dens is common in several species of rattlesnakes in areas where winters are harsh enough to require snakes to hibernate. This is the case in the northern three-quarters of Texas, that is, north of the southern margin of the Hill Country (Balcones Escarpment). Dens provide the necessary temperature and moisture conditions for rattlesnakes (and a surprising variety of other animals) to survive the winter, and may serve at other times as places for mating and giving birth. A limited number of den sites support local rattlesnake populations in any given area, so the use of dens for any of the activities mentioned above concentrates snakes in a few places, making it easier to adversely affect populations at such times through unrestricted harvesting. The effects of such adverse impacts on rattlesnakes may be significant, since relatively few females normally survive to reproductive age and those then produce relatively few young. We don't know how significant these adverse impacts may be in Texas, however, because the relevant data have not been collected.

Readers who do not already know that gasoline fumes are toxic can readily demonstrate that fact for themselves. It should therefore come as no surprise that gasoline fumes sprayed into a confined space may kill various animals living therein, depending on the architecture of the den and the ability of the animals to escape the fumes. I do not think this practice will result in some regional environmental catastrophe, but I am reasonably confident that pollution levels at local den sites treated this way will increase through time. We simply do not know whether or how such practices affect the long-term suitability of individual sites as dens, and so neither do we know the effects upon the social structure and life-history patterns of local rattlesnake populations.

The western diamondback rattlesnake, representing the vast majority of rattlesnakes harvested for commercial purposes in Texas, is widespread and abundant. There is no reason in theory why this species can't be harvested sustainably as long as other wildlife species continue to be. Texans have, however, been harvesting this animal for some time without studying the effect of doing so on the long-term sustainability of local populations. We have been conducting an experiment but gathering little data, and the experiment has been "designed" to render the data that have been taken useless for answering the questions asked. In other words, we have no idea how mortality from all sources is affecting rattlesnake populations in Texas. We can continue to assume they are doing just fine, but similar assumptions for other species under similar circumstances in the past have proved to be wrong.

We are left to decide whether it is important to design and carry out the proper studies and experiments necessary to answer the questions posed above. I think it is, obviously, but I am arguing a particular viewpoint. I want to know that rattlesnakes, which form such an integral weave in the fabric of life in Texas, can continue to be used responsibly by future generations of Texans. I hope enough of us can embrace my position to make it a reality.

USEFUL SOURCES OF INFORMATION

South Texas Poison Center
University of Texas Health Science Center at San Antonio
Room 146, Forensic Science Building
7703 Floyd Curl Drive
San Antonio, TX 78284-7849
210-567-5762

Central Texas Poison Center
Scott and White Memorial Hospital
2401 S. 31st St.
Temple, TX 76508
817-724-7403

North Texas Poison Center
P.O. Box 35926
5201 Harry Hines Boulevard
Dallas, TX 75235
214-589-0911

Southeast Texas Poison Center
Clinical Pharmacology and Toxicology Unit
University of Texas Medical Branch
301 University Boulevard
Galveston, TX 77555-1031
409-772-9612

West Texas Regional Poison Center
4800 Alameda Avenue
El Paso, TX 79905
915-534-3800

Panhandle Poison Center
1501 S. Coulter
Amarillo, TX 79106
806-354-1630

Arizona Poison and Drug Information Center
University of Arizona
1501 N. Campbell Avenue
Tucson, AZ 85724
520-626-6016

Therapeutic Antibodies, Inc.
1207 17th Avenue S., #103
Nashville, TN 37212

Wyeth International Laboratories, Ltd.
P. O. Box 8299
Philadelphia, PA 19101
717-426-1941

GLOSSARY

ANAPHYLAXIS hypersensitivity to a foreign substance, resulting in a severe or fatal systemic breakdown characterized by respiratory distress, fainting, itching, and skin rashes.

ANTICOAGULANT a substance that prevents blood from clotting.

APICAL of or pertaining to the posterior tip of the dorsal scales.

ARTHROPOD any member of the phylum Arthropoda, characterized by segmented bodies and jointed legs and including insects, arachnids, and crustaceans.

BAJADA (Spanish, "down below") a name given to an alluvial outwash slope extending from the mouth of a canyon downward to an intermountain basin in many parts of the desert Southwest.

CLADE in phylogenetic systematics (the classification of organisms based on ancestor-descendant relationships), a group of organisms with a common ancestor.

CONGENER a species that is a member of the same genus as another.

CONSPECIFIC an individual organism that is a member of the same species as another.

CREPUSCULAR active primarily at twilight or dawn.

CRYPSIS the ability of an organism to escape detection through a combination of behavior and camouflage.

CYANOSIS a bluish black discoloration around a bite area, resulting from a significant breakdown of local tissue.

DALTONS an atomic mass unit equal to one-twelfth of the mass of an atom of carbon-12; approximately 1.6598×10^{-24} grams.

DEBRIDEMENT the surgical removal of dead or infected tissue.

DEFIBRINATION the condition in which plasma fibrinogen, an important component of the blood-clotting mechanism, is absent.

DORSAL of or pertaining to the upper surface of the body.

ECCHYMOSIS severe discoloration of the skin resulting from ruptured blood vessels leaking blood into surrounding tissue.

FASCICULATIONS small, local, involuntary muscular contractions visible under the skin, most noticeably in the area of a bite as well as on the face and over the large muscle groups of the back and neck, representing the spontaneous discharge by motor neurons responding to the action of several venom components.

5′-NUCLEOTIDASE an enzyme that specifically acts to break the bond between the 5′ end of a nucleotide and its phosphate group; the net result is the destruction of the functional integrity of a DNA or RNA molecule.

GENERA plural of genus, the category just above the species level in the Linnaean taxonomic hierarchy.

GLYCOURIA the presence of excess glucose in the urine.

GRAVID pregnant or containing a mass of enlarged eggs almost ready to lay.

HEMATEMESIS the vomiting of blood.

HEMATURIA the discharge of blood in the urine.

HEMOLYTIC causing the destruction or dissolution of red blood cells.

HEMORRHAGIC causing the extensive destruction of endothelial cells in blood vessels.

HIBERNACULA plural of *hibernaculum*; places where animals seek shelter before entering a state of decreased physiological activity during the winter.

HYALURONIDASE an enzyme that hydrolyzes hyaluronic acid, causing connective tissue to dissociate and thereby to lose its functional integrity; when this happens, venom components reach target tissues and organ systems more quickly; also called "spreading factor."

HYPOTENSIVE of or pertaining to low blood pressure.

IP intraperitoneal; refers to the injection of a substance into the body cavity of a vertebrate.

IV intravenous; refers to the injection of a substance into the circulatory system of a vertebrate.

IMMUNOASSAY the identification of a substance such as a protein through its ability to provoke an immune response.

INFRALABIAL below the lower line of the mouth.

INTERSUPRAOCULAR SCALE a scale on top of the head, lying between the supraocular scales.

ISOFORM one of several three-dimensional configurations that a specific molecule may take.

KEELED pertaining to scales with an elevated, longitudinal ridge that may or may not extend from base to tip, and may be either sharp and well defined or broad and obtuse.

LD$_{50}$ the venom dosage, expressed as milligrams of venom per kilogram of the test animal (usually laboratory mice), that is lethal to 50% of the experimental subjects during a twenty-four-hour period in a clinical trial.

LOREAL SCALE a scale located on either side of the head and between the preocular scales and the postnasal scale.

LYRE a stringed musical instrument similar to a harp; on some snakes, refers to dorsal head markings that suggest the shape of this instrument.

MELENA the presence of blood in feces.

MYOLYTIC causing the disintegration or liquefaction of muscle tissue.

NECROSIS tissue death; can be followed by gangrene and may necessitate amputation if left untreated; largely preventable with appropriate antivenom therapy.

NEUROTOXIN a toxin that primarily or exclusively affects the nervous system.

PARIETAL SCALE a scale lying on top of the head behind the supraocular scales.

PEPTIDE a protein subunit consisting of multiple amino acids joined together by amide bonds.

PHOSPHOLIPASE an enzyme that hydrolyzes phospholipids, which are major components of biological membranes.

POSTOCULAR behind the eye.

PREFOVEAL SCALE one of the small scales surrounding the opening of the infrared receptor on each side of the face of pit vipers.

PREOCULAR SCALE the scale immediately in front of the eye.

PROTEASE a general class of enzymes that break up proteins into smaller subunits.

PROTEINURIA the presence of excess serum protein in the urine.

PROTEOLYTIC causing the destruction or dissociation of proteins through the hydrolysis of peptide bonds.

RHOMBOID a four-sided shape, each side equal in length, with the diagonally opposite angles equal to each other, and two angles being acute and two obtuse.

ROSTRAL SCALE the scale forming the tip of the snout.

SC subcutaneous; refers to the injection of a substance beneath the surface skin layers but not directly into the circulatory system or body cavity of a vertebrate.

SARCOLEMMA the thin membrane enclosing striated muscle fibers.

SCALE ROW a longitudinal series of dorsal or lateral scales.

SEXUAL DIMORPHISM the condition of diagnostic morphological differences existing between the sexes within a species.

SUBCAUDAL SCALES the scales that cover the underside of the tail.

SUPRAOCULAR SCALE the large plate that lies above the eye.

SYMPHYSES plural of *symphysis*; the cartilaginous joints between two bones.

TALUS an accumulation of rock fragments below steep slopes or cliffs.

TRANSVERSE perpendicular to the long axis of the body.

UNDULATING furnished with wave-like markings.

VENTRAL of or pertaining to the lower surface of the body.

VESICULATIONS swellings of the skin filled with clear serous fluid or blood; in snakebites, usually occurring in the vicinity of the bite, but can involve an entire extremity in serious cases.

REFERENCES

Adams, C. E., J. K. Thomas, K. J. Strnadel, and S. L. Jester. 1994. Texas
 rattlesnake roundups: Implications of unregulated commercial
 use of wildlife. Wlldl. Soc. Bull. 22 (2): 324–330.

Alexander, H. L., Jr. 1963. The Levi site: A paleo-Indian campsite in
 central Texas. Amer. Antiquity 28 (4): 510–528.

Allen, J. A. 1896. On mammals collected in Bexar County and
 vicinity, Texas, by Mr. H. P. Attwater, with field notes by the
 collector. Bull. Amer. Mus. Nat. Hist. 8:47–80.

Allen, R. P. 1952. *The whooping crane*. National Audubon Society
 Resource Report 3. New York: National Audubon Society.

Beaupre, S. J. 1995. Comparative ecology of the mottled rock
 rattlesnake, *Crotalus lepidus*, in Big Bend National Park.
 Herpetologica 51 (1): 45–56.

Beavers, R. A. 1976. Food habits of the western diamondback
 rattlesnake, *Crotalus atrox*, in Texas. Southwest. Nat. 20 (4):
 503–515.

Beckers, G. J. L., T. A. A. M. Leenders, and H. Strijbosch. 1996. Coral
 snake mimicry: Live snakes not avoided by a mammalian
 predator. Oecologia 106 (4): 461–463.

Bent, A. C. 1926. *Life histories of North American marsh birds.* U.S. National Museum Bulletin 135. Washington, D.C.: GPO.

Bergstrom, P. W. 1988. Breeding displays and vocalizations of Wilson's plovers. Wilson Bull. 100:36–49.

Black, S. L. 1978. *Archaeological investigations at the Banquete Bend Site (41 NU 63) Nueces County, Texas.* Archaeological Survey Report 63. San Antonio: Univ. of Texas at San Antonio, Center for Archaeological Research.

Blair, W. F. 1954. Mammals of the mesquite plains biotic district in Texas and Oklahoma, and speciation in the central grasslands. Texas J. Sci. 6 (3): 235–264.

Boundy, J. 1995. Maximum lengths of North American snakes. Bull. Chicago Herpetol. Soc. 30 (6): 109–122.

Brodie, E. D., III, and F. J. Janzen. 1995. Experimental studies of coral snake mimicry: Generalized avoidance of ringed snake patterns by free-ranging avian predators. Funct. Ecol. 9 (2): 186–190.

Brooks, J. L. 2005. The role of covey demographics in northern bobwhite (*Colinus virginianus*) production. MS thesis, Texas A&M Univ.

Brown, B. C. 1955. The herpetology of the coastal prairie region of Texas. PhD diss., Univ. of Michigan.

Brown, D. O., ed. 1987. *Archeology at Aquilla Lake, 1978–1982: Investigations.* Vol. III. Research Report 81. Austin: University of Texas, Texas Archaeological Survey.

Brown, W. S. 1993. *Biology, status, and management of the timber rattlesnake (Crotalus horridus): A guide for conservation.* Herpetological Circular 22. Lawrence, Kan.: Society for the Study of Amphibians and Reptiles.

Buntyn, R. J. 2004. Reproductive ecology and survival of scaled quail in the Trans-Pecos region of Texas. MS thesis, Angelo State Univ.

Burkett, R.D. 1966. Natural history of cottonmouth moccasin, *Agkistrodon piscivorus* (Reptilia). Univ. Kansas Publ. Mus. Nat. Hist. 17 (9): 435–491.

Butler, B. H. 1979. Faunal remains from Coleto Creek, Goliad County, Texas [Appendix I]. In *Archaeological investigations of two prehistoric sites on the Coleto Creek drainage, Goliad County, Texas*, ed. D. E. Fox, 83–100. Archaeological Survey Report 69. San Antonio: Univ. of Texas at San Antonio, Center for Archaeological Research.

Campbell, J. A., and E. D. Brodie, Jr., eds. 1992. *Biology of the pit vipers*. Tyler, Tex.: Selva.

Campbell, J. A., D. R. Formanowicz, Jr., and E. D. Brodie, Jr. 1989. Potential impact of rattlesnake roundups on natural populations. Texas J. Sci. 41 (3): 301–317.

Campbell, J. A., and W. W. Lamar. 2004. *The venomous reptiles of the Western Hemisphere*. Ithaca, N.Y.: Cornell Univ. Press.

Carpenter, C. C., and J. C. Gillingham. 1975. Postural responses to kingsnakes by crotaline snakes. Herpetologica 31 (3): 293–302.

Carpenter, C. C., J. C. Gillingham, and J. B. Murphy. 1976. The combat ritual of the rock rattlesnake (*Crotalus lepidus*). Copeia, 1976 (4): 764–780.

Casner, P. R., and M. J. Zuckerman. 1990. *Salmonella arizonae* in patients with AIDS along the U.S.-Mexican border. New England J. Med. 323:198–199.

Chadderdon, M. F. 1983. Baker Cave, Val Verde County, Texas: The 1976 investigations. Research Special Report 13. San Antonio: Univ. of Texas at San Antonio, Center for Archaeological Research.

Chiszar, D., R. Conant, and H. M. Smith. 2003. Observations on the rattlesnake *Crotalus atrox* by Berlandier, 1829–1851. Bull. Chicago Herpetol. Soc. 38 (7): 138–142.

Clark, R. F. 1949. Snakes of the hill parishes of Louisiana. J. Tennessee Acad. Sci. 24 (4): 244–261.

Coffman, R. J. 1986. Vertebrate faunal remains at the Kenyon Rockshelter, 41TV742 [Appendix C]. In *Cultural ecology of the Kenyon Rockshelter and the Cunningham Site, Canyon Creek Development, Travis County, Texas (Reports of Investigations)*, ed. R. J. Coffman, M. C. Trachte, and M. B. Collins, 383–402. Austin: Prewitt and Associates Report of Investigations.

Collins, M. B. 1969. *Test excavations at Amistad International Reservoir, fall, 1967*. Misc. Paper 16. Austin: Univ. of Texas, Texas Archaeological Salvage Project.

Collins, R. F., and C. C. Carpenter. 1970. Organ position-ventral scute relationship in the water moccasin (*Agkistrodon piscivorus leucostoma*), with notes on food habits and distribution. Proc. Oklahoma Acad. Sci. 49:15–18.

Cone, L. A., W. H. Boughton, L. A. Cone, and L. H. Lehv. 1990. Rattlesnake capsule-induced *Salmonella arizonae* bacteremia. Western J. Med. 153 (3): 315–316.

Cottam, C., W. C. Glazener, and G. G. Raun. 1959. *Notes on food of moccasins and rattlesnakes from the Welder Wildlife Refuge, Sinton, Texas*. Sinton, Tex.: Welder Wildlife Foundation.

Cottam, C., and J. B. Trefethan, eds. 1968. *Whitewings: The life history, status, and management of the white-winged dove*. Princeton, N.J.: Van Nostrand.

Creel, D. 1990. *Excavations at 41TG91, Tom Green County, Texas, 1978*. Publications in Archaeology, Report 38. Austin: Texas Department of Transportation, Design Division.

Creel, D., R. F. Scott, IV, and M. B. Collins. 1990. A faunal record from west central Texas and its bearing on Late Holocene bison population changes in the southern plains. Plains Anthropol. 35:55–69.

Crimmins, M. L. 1931. Rattlesnakes and their enemies in the southwest. Bull. Antivenin Inst. Amer. 5 (2): 46–47.

———. 1946. The rattlesnake in the art and life of the American Indian. Bull. Texas Archeol. Paleontol. Soc. 17:28–41.

Crouse, H. W. 1902. The venomous snakes and spiders of Texas. Trans. Texas St. Med. Assoc. 34:1–39.

Curtis, L. 1949. The snakes of Dallas County, Texas. Field Lab. 17 (1): 5–12.

———. 1952. Cannibalism in the Texas coral snake. Herpetologica 8:27.

Dalquest, W. W. 1962. The Good Creek formation, Pleistocene of Texas, and its fauna. J. Paleontol. 36 (3): 568–582.

Daniels, R. L. 1976. Preliminary excavations at the Randig Site, Williamson County, Texas. J. So. Texas Archaeol. Assoc. 3 (4): 21–28.

Davis, R. B., C. F. Herreid, II, and H. L. Short. 1962. Mexican free-tailed bats in Texas. Ecol. Monogr. 32:311–346.

Davis, W. B. 1938. White-throated sparrow killed by copperhead. Condor 40:183.

———. 1951. Eastern moles eaten by cottonmouth and gray fox. J. Mamm. 32:114–115.

Dawson, E. T. 1955. *Texas wildlife*. Dallas: Banks, Upshaw.

DeMarcay, G. B. 1986. Vertebrate fauna from Landergin Mesa: An Antelope Creek Period village site. MA thesis, Texas A&M Univ.

Dickerman, R. W., and C. W. Painter. 2001. Natural history notes: *Crotalus lepidus lepidus* (mottled rock rattlesnake). Diet. Herpetol. Rev. 32 (1): 46.

Dillehay, T.D., and B. M. Davidson. 1975. Statistical data on faunal remains from excavated sites in the Wallisville Reservoir, 1973 season [Appendix IV]. In *Prehistoric subsistence exploitation in the lower Trinity River Delta, Texas*, ed. T. D. Dillehay, 163–179. Research Report 51. Austin: University of Texas, Texas Archaeological Survey.

Dixon, J. R. 1987. *Amphibians and reptiles of Texas, with keys, taxonomic synopses, bibliography, and distribution maps.* College Station: Texas A&M Univ. Press.

Dobie, J. F. 1965. *Rattlesnakes.* New York: Little, Brown.

Doehner, K., D. Peter, and S. A. Skinner. 1978. *Evaluation of the archaeology at the proposed Cooper Lake.* Archaeological Research Program, Research Report 114. Dallas: Southern Methodist Univ.

Duvall, D., M. J. Goode, W. K. Hayes, J. K. Leonhardt, and D. G. Brown. 1990. Prairie rattlesnake vernal migration: Field experimental analyses and survival value. Natl. Geogr. Res. 6 (4): 457–469.

Duvall, D., M. B. King, and K. J. Gutzwiller. 1985. Behavioral ecology and ethology of the prairie rattlesnake. Natl. Geogr. Res. 1 (1): 80–111.

Eads, R. B., J. S. Wiseman, and G. C. Menzies. 1957. Observations concerning the Mexican free-tailed bat, *Tadarida mexicana*, in Texas. Texas J. Sci. 9 (2): 227–242.

Edmonds, S. T., and D. S. Stolley. 2008. Population decline of ground-nesting black-bellied whistling ducks (*Dendrocygna autumnalis*) on islands in southern Texas. Southwest. Nat. 53 (2): 185–189.

Elliott, W. R., and J. R. Reddell. 1975. The fauna of the Devil's Sinkhole. In *Devil's Sinkhole area--headwaters of the Nueces River: A natural area survey*, ed. D. Kennard, 70–74. Austin: University of Texas.

Ernst, C. H. 1992. *Venomous reptiles of North America.* Washington, D.C.: Smithsonian Institution Press.

Fainstein, V., R. Yancey, P. Trier, and G. P. Bodey. 1982. Overwhelming infection in a cancer patient caused by *Arizona hinshawii*: Its relation to snake pill ingestion. Amer. J. Infect. Contr. 10:147–148.

Fedigan, L. 1974. The classification of predators by Japanese macaques (*Macaca fuscata*) in the mesquite-chapparal habitat of south Texas. Amer. J. Phys. Anthropol. 40:135.

Few, J., R. Brewington, K. E. Fustes, W. L. McClure, and B. Penhaker. 2002. Investigations at the Follet Lake Site (41BO138): The 1994 and 1995 TAS field schools. Bull. Texas Archaeol. Soc. 73:99–114.

Fiero, M. K., M. W. Seifert, T. J. Weaver, and C. A. Bonilla. 1972. Comparative study of juvenile and adult prairie rattlesnake (*Crotalus viridis viridis*) venoms. Toxicon 10:81–82.

Fitch, H. S. 1960. Autecology of the copperhead. Univ. Kansas Publ. Mus. Nat. Hist. 13 (4): 85–288.

Fitzgerald, L. A., and C. W. Painter. 2000. Rattlesnake commercialization: Long-term trends, issues, and implications for conservation. Wildl. Soc. Bull. 28 (1): 235–253.

Fleet, R. R., and J. C. Kroll. 1978. Litter size and parturition behavior in *Sistrurus miliarius streckeri*. Herpetol. Rev. 9:11.

Flynn, L. M. 1983. Faunal analysis: 41 GD 30A [Appendix II]. In *The Berger Bluff site (41 GD 30A): Excavations in the upper deposits, 1979*, ed. D. O. Brown, 104–122. Archaeological Survey Report 115. San Antonio: Univ. of Texas at San Antonio, Center for Archaeological Research.

Ford, N. B. 2002. Ecology of the western cottonmouth (*Agkistrodon piscivorus leucostoma*) in northeastern Texas. In *Biology of the vipers*, ed. G. W. Schuett, M. Höggren, M. E. Douglas, and H. W. Greene, 167–177. Eagle Mountain, Utah: Eagle Mountain Publishing.

Ford, N. B., F. Brischoux, and D. Lancaster. 2004. Reproduction in the western cottonmouth, *Agkistrodon piscivorus leucostoma*, in a floodplain forest. Southwest. Nat. 49 (4): 465–471.

Ford, N. B., V. A. Cobb, and W. W. Lamar. 1990. Reproductive data on snakes from northeastern Texas. Texas J. Sci. 42 (4): 355–368.

Forks, J. E., and T. M. Hughes. 2007. *Crotalus molossus molossus* (northern black–tailed rattlesnake) diet. Herpetol. Rev. 38 (2): 205.

Forstner, M. R. J., R. A. Hilsenbeck, and J. F. Scudday. 1997. Geographic variation in whole venom profiles from the mottled rock rattlesnake (*Crotalus lepidus lepidus*) in Texas. J. Herpetol. 31 (2): 277–287.

Fouquette, M. J., Jr. and H. L. Lindsay, Jr. 1955. An ecological survey of reptiles in parts of northwestern Texas. Texas J. Sci. 7:402–421.

Fox, A. A. 1998. Artifacts and faunal material. In *Archaeological and historical investigations at Rancho de las Cabras, 41WN30, Wilson County, Texas: Fourth season*, ed. A. A. Fox and B. A.

Houk, 20–26. Archaeological Survey Report 143. San Antonio: Univ. of Texas at San Antonio, Center for Archaeological Research.

Fox, A. A., F. A. Bass, Jr., and T. R. Hester. 1977. *The archaeology and history of Alamo Plaza*. Archaeological Survey Report 16. San Antonio: Univ. of Texas at San Antonio, Center for Archaeological Research.

Fox, A. A., S. L. Black, and S. R. James. 1979. *Intensive survey and testing of archaeological sites on Coleto Creek, Victoria and Goliad counties, Texas*. Archaeological Survey Report 67. San Antonio: Univ. of Texas at San Antonio, Center for Archaeological Research.

Fox, A. A., and S. A. Tomka. 2006. Excavations at Presidio Nuestra Señora de Loreto de la Bahía del Espíritu Santo. Bull. Texas Archaeol. Soc. 77–159.

Fox, D. E., R. J. Mallouf, N. O'Malley, and W. M. Sorrow. 1974. *Archaeological resources of the proposed Cuero I Reservoir, DeWitt and Gonzales counties, Texas*. Archaeological Survey Report 12. Austin: Texas Historical Commission and Texas Water Development Board.

Fox, D. E., E. H. Schmiedlin, and J. L. Mitchell. 1978. Preliminary report on the J-2 Ranch Site (41 VT 6), Victoria County, Texas. La Tierra 5 (3): 2–14.

Frederiksen, J. K., and C. N. Slobodchikoff. 2007. Referential specificity in the alarm calls of the black-tailed prairie dog. Ethol. Ecol. Evol. 19:87–99.

Freeman, B. 2003. White-tailed hawk immunities. Texas Ornithology Listserv. 2003 (3):1.

Froehlich, L. 2002. Identification of faunal remains [Appendix H]. In *The Smith Creek Bridge site (41DW270): A terrace site in De Witt County, Texas*, ed. D. Hudler, K. Prilliman, and T. Gustavson, 283–337. Austin: Univ. of Texas, Texas Archaeological Research Laboratory.

Garcia, V. E., and J. C. Perez. 1984. The purification and characterization of an antihemorrhagic factor in woodrat (*Neotoma micropus*) serum. Toxicon 22:129–138.

Gehlbach, F. R. [1956] 1957. Annotated records of southwestern amphibians and reptiles. Trans. Kansas Acad. Sci. 59:364–372.

———. 1970. Death-feigning and erratic behavior in leptotyphlopid, colubrid, and elapid snakes. Herpetologica 26 (1): 24–34.

———. 1972. Coral snake mimicry reconsidered: The strategy of self-mimicry. Forma Functio 5:311–320.

Gehlbach, F. R., and J. A. Holman. 1974. Paleoecology of amphibians and reptiles from Pratt Cave, Guadalupe Mountains National Park, Texas. Southwest. Nat. 19 (2): 191–198.

Gibbons, J. W., and M. E. Dorcas. 2002. Defensive behavior of cottonmouths (*Agkistrodon piscivorus*) toward humans. Copeia, 2002 (1): 195–198.

Gillingham, J. C., and R. E. Baker. 1981. Evidence for scavenging behavior in the western diamondback rattlesnake (*Crotalus atrox*). Z. Tierpsychol. 55 (3): 217–227.

Gillingham, J. C., C. C. Carpenter, and J. B. Murphy. 1983. Courtship, male combat and dominance in the western diamondback rattlesnake, *Crotalus atrox*. J. Herpetol. 17 (3): 265–270.

Giovanni, M. D., C. A. Taylor, and G. Perry. 2005. *Crotalus viridis viridis* (prairie rattlesnake) diet. Herpetol. Rev. 36 (3): 323.

Glass, T. G., Jr.. 1976. *Management of poisonous snakebite.* San Antonio: privately printed.

Glaudas, X. 2004. Do cottonmouths (*Agkistrodon piscivorus*) habituate to human confrontations? Southeast. Nat. 3 (1): 129–138.

Glenn, J. L., and R. C. Straight. 1978. Mojave rattlesnake *Crotalus scutulatus scutulatus* venom: Variation in toxicity with geographical origin. Toxicon 16:81–84.

———. 1982. The rattlesnakes and their venom yield and lethal toxicity. *In Rattlesnake venoms: Their actions and treatment*, ed. A. T. Tu, 3–119. New York: Dekker.

Glenn, J. L., R. C. Straight, M. C. Wolfe, and D. L. Hardy. 1983. Geographical variation in *Crotalus scutulatus scutulatus* (Mojave rattlesnake) venom properties. Toxicon 21 (1): 119–130.

Glenn, J. L., R. C. Straight, and T. B. Wolt. 1994. Regional variation in the presence of canebrake toxin in *Crotalus horridus* venom. Comp. Biochem. Physiol. 107C (3): 337–346.

Gloyd, H. K. 1948. Another account of the "dance" of the western diamondback rattlesnake. Nat. Hist. Misc. 34:1–3.

———. 1958. Aberrations in the color patterns of some crotalid snakes. Bull. Chicago Acad. Sci. 10 (12): 185–195.

Gloyd, H. K., and R. Conant. 1990. *Snakes of the "Agkistrodon" complex: A monographic review.* Oxford, Ohio: Society for the Study of Amphibians and Reptiles.

Goldberg, S. R. 1999. Reproduction in the blacktail rattlesnake, *Crotalus molossus* (Serpentes: Viperidae). Texas J. Sci. 51 (4): 323–328.

———. 1999 [2000]. Reproduction in the rock rattlesnake, *Crotalus lepidus* (Serpentes: Viperidae). Herpetol. Nat. Hist. 7:83–86.

Goldberg, S. R., and P. C. Rosen. 2000. Reproduction in the mojave rattlesnake, *Crotalus scutulatus* (Serpentes: Viperidae). Texas J. Sci. 52 (2): 101–109.

Goodrum, P. D. 1967. The gray squirrel in Texas. Bull. Texas Parks Wildl. Dept. 42:1–43.

Graves, B. M., and D. Duvall. 1993. Reproduction, rookery use, and thermoregulation in free-ranging, pregnant *Crotalus v. viridis*. J. Herpetol. 27 (1): 33–41.

Greding, E. J., Jr. 1964. Food of *Ancistrodon c. concortrix* in Houston and Trinity counties, Texas. Southwest. Nat. 9:105.

Green, L. M., and F. O. Green. 1974. Notes on the archaeology of the Allen Ranch rock shelters, Terrell County, Texas. Artifact 12 (1).

Greene, H. W. 1973. The food habits and feeding behavior of New World coral snakes. MA thesis, Univ. of Texas at Arlington.

———. 1997. *Snakes: The evolution of mystery in nature.* Berkeley and Los Angeles: Univ. of California Press.

Greene, H. W., and R. W. McDiarmid. 1981. Coral snake mimicry: Does it occur? Science 213:1207–1212.

Greene, H. W., and G. V. Oliver, Jr. 1965. Notes on the natural history of the western massasauga. Herpetologica 21 (3): 225–228.

Griffen, D., and J. W. Donovan. 1986. Significant envenomation from a preserved rattlesnake head (in a patient with a history of immediate hypersensitivity to antivenin). Ann. Emerg. Med. 15:955–958.

Guidry, E. V. 1953. Herpetological notes from southeastern Texas. Herpetologica 9:49–56.

Haines, A. M., M. E. Tewes, and L. L. Laack. 2005. Survival and sources of mortality in ocelots. J. Wildl. Manag. 69 (1): 255–263.

Harris, E. S. 1985. *An archaeological study of the Timmeron Rockshelter (41 HY 95), Hays County, south central Texas.* Special Publication 4. San Antonio: Southern Texas Archaeological Association.

Hartline, P. H., L. Kass, and M. S. Loop. 1978. Merging of modalities in the optic tectum: Infrared and visual integration in rattlesnakes. Science 199:1225–1229.

Hartman, C. 1922. A brown rat kills a rattler. J. Mamm. 3 (2): 116–117.

Headrick, P. 1993. *The archaeology of 41NU11, the Kirchmeyer Site, Nueces County, Texas: Long-term utilization of a coastal clay dune.* Studies in Archaeology 15. Austin: Univ. of Texas, Texas Archaeological Research Laboratory.

Hecht, M. K., and D. Marien. 1956. The coral snake mimic problem: A reinterpretation. J. Morphol. 98 (2): 335–365.

Hellier, J. R., D. G. Steele, and C. A. Hunter. 1995. Analysis of nonhuman vertebrate faunal remains [Appendix C]. In vol. 2 of *Archeological investigations at the Loma Sandia site (41LK28): A prehistoric cemetery and campsite in Live Oak County, Texas,* ed. A. J. Taylor and C. L. Highley, 801–828. Studies in Archaeology 20. Austin: Univ. of Texas, Texas Archaeological Research Laboratory.

Herreid, C. F., II. 1961. Snakes as predators of bats. Herpetologica 17 (4): 271–272.

Hester, T. R. 1975. Late prehistoric cultural patterns along the lower Rio Grande of Texas. Bull. Texas Archeol. Soc. 46:107–125.

———. 1977. *Archaeological research at the Hinojosa Site (41 JW 8), Jim Wells County, southern Texas.* Archaeological Survey Report 42. San Antonio: Univ. of Texas at San Antonio, Center for Archaeological Research.

———. 1978. *Studies in the archaeology of Chaparrosa Ranch.* Vol. 1: *Background to the archaeology of Chaparrosa Ranch, southern Texas.* Special Report 6. San Antonio: Univ. of Texas at San Antonio, Center for Archaeological Research.

———. 1983 [1982]. Late Paleo-Indian occupations at Baker Cave, southwestern Texas. Bull. Texas Archaeol. Soc. 53:101–119.

Hester, T. R., and T. C. Hill, Jr. 1973. Prehistoric occupation of the Holdsworth and Stewart sites on the Rio Grande Plain of Texas. Bull. Texas Archaeol. Soc. 43:33–65.

———. 1975. Some aspects of late prehistoric and protohistoric archaeology in southern Texas. Special Report 1. San Antonio: Univ. of Texas at San Antonio, Center for Archaeological Research.

Highley, L., C. Graves, C. Land, and G. Judson. 1978. Archaeological investigations at Scorpion Cave (41 ME 7) Medina County, Texas. Bull. Texas Archaeol. Soc. 49:139–194.

Hill, W. H. 1971. Pleistocene snakes from a cave in Kendall County, Texas. Texas J. Sci. 22 (2–3): 209–216.

Hinman, K. E., H. L. Throop, K. L. Adams, A. J. Dake, K. K. McLauchlan, and M. J. McKone. 1997. Predation by free-ranging birds on partial coral snake mimics: The importance of ring width and color. Evolution 51 (3): 1011–1014.

Holman, J. A. 1963. Late Pleistocene amphibians and reptiles of the Clear Creek and Ben Franklin local faunas of Texas. J. Grad. Res. Center 31:152–167.

———. 1964. Pleistocene amphibians and reptiles from Texas. Herpetologica 20 (2): 73–83.

Holman, J. A., and A. J. Winkler. 1987. A mid-Pleistocene (Irvingtonian) herpetofauna from a cave in south central Texas. Pearce-Sellards Ser. 44:1–17.

Holmback, E. 1981. Crotalus atrox (western diamondback rattlesnake) coloration. Herpetol. Rev. 12:70.

———. 1985. Crotalus atrox (western diamondback rattlesnake) coloration. Herpetol. Rev. 16:78.

Hudson, W. R., Jr., W. M. Lynn, and D. Scurlock. 1974. Walker Ranch: An archaeological reconnaissance and excavations in northern Bexar County, Texas. Office of the State Archaeologist Report 26. Austin: Texas Historical Commission.

Hulbert, R. C., Jr. 1985. Vertebrate faunal remains. In The Panther Springs Creek site: Cultural change and continuity within the Upper Salado Creek watershed, south-central Texas, ed. S. L. Black and A. J. McGraw, 209–215. Archaeological Survey Report 100. San Antonio: Univ. of Texas at San Antonio, Center for Archaeological Research.

Hunter, C. A. 2001. Vertebrate faunal remains. In Prehistory of the Rustler Hills: Granado Cave, ed. D. L. Hamilton, 225–236. Austin: Univ. of Texas Press.

Ivey, J. E., and A. A. Fox. 1981. Archaeological survey and testing at Rancho de las Cabras, Wilson County, Texas. Archaeological Survey Report 104. San Antonio: Univ. of Texas at San Antonio, Center for Archaeological Research.

Jacob, J. S. 1977. An evaluation of the possibility of hybridization between the rattlesnakes Crotalus atrox and C. scutulatus in the southwestern United States. Southwest. Nat. 22 (4): 469–485.

Jameson, D. L. 1955. The population dynamics of the cliff frog, Syrrhophus marnocki. Amer. Midl. Nat. 54 (2): 342–381.

Johnson, E. 1986. Late Pleistocene and Early Holocene vertebrates and paleoenvironments of the Southern High Plains, U.S.A. Geogr. physiq. Quatern. 40 (3): 249–261.

———. 1987. Vertebrate remains. In *Lubbock Lake: Late Quaternary studies on the Southern High Plains*, ed. E. Johnson, 49–89. College Station: Texas A&M Univ. Press.

Johnson, E., V.T. Holliday, M.J. Kaczor, and R. Stuckenrath. 1977. The Garza Occupation at the Lubbock Lake Site. Bull. Texas Archaeol. Soc. 48:83–109.

Jurgens, C. J. 2005. Zooarchaeology and bone technology from Arenosa Shelter (41VV99), lower Pecos region, Texas. PhD diss., Univ. of Texas.

Karges, J. P. 1979. An aberrant pattern morph in a western diamondback rattlesnake, *Crotalus atrox*, from southern Texas. Trans. Kansas Acad. Sci. 82 (4): 205–208.

Keck, M. B. 1998. Habitat use by semi-aquatic snakes at ponds on a reclaimed strip mine. Southwest. Nat. 43 (1): 13–19.

Kegley, G. 1980. *Archaeological investigations at Hueco Tanks State Park, El Paso County, Texas.* Austin: Texas Parks and Wildlife Department, Parks Division, Interpretations and Exhibits Branch.

Kendall, G. W. 1844. *Narrative of the Texan Santa Fé expedition. Comprising a description of a tour through Texas, and across the great southwestern prairies, the Camanche and Caygüa hunting-grounds, with an account of the sufferings from want of food, losses from hostile Indians, and final capture of the Texans. And their march, as prisoners, to the City of Mexico.* Vol. I. London: Wiley & Putnam.

Kennedy, J. P. 1964. Natural history notes on some snakes of eastern Texas. Texas J. Sci. 16 (2): 210–215.

Keyler, D. E., and K. Schwitzer. 1987. Envenomation from the fang of a freeze-dried prairie rattlesnake head. Vet. Hum. Toxicol. 29 (6): 440–441.

Killebrew, F. C., and T. L. James. 1983. *Crotalus viridis viridis* (prairie rattlesnake) coloration. Herpetol. Rev. 14 (3): 74.

Kilmon, J., and H. Shelton. 1981. *Rattlesnakes in America. Part I: A biology of the rattlesnakes and their impact on human society. Part II: A history of the Sweetwater Jaycees rattlesnake roundup.* Sweetwater, Tex.: Shelton Press.

King, K. A. 1975. Unusual food item of the western diamondback rattlesnake (*Crotalus atrox*). Southwest. Nat. 20 (3): 416–417.

King, M. B., and D. Duvall. 1990. Prairie rattlesnake seasonal migrations: Episodes of movement, vernal foraging and sex differences. Anim. Behav. 39 (5): 924–935.

Klauber, L. M. 1972. *Rattlesnakes: Their habits, life histories, and influence on mankind.* 2 vols. Berkeley and Los Angeles: Univ. of California Press.

Knopf, G. N., and D. W. Tinkle. 1961. The distribution and habits of *Sistrurus catenatus* in northwest Texas. Herpetologica 17 (2): 126–131.

Kostecke, R. M., S. G. Summers, J. W. Bailey, and D. A. Cimprich. 2004. Confirmed nesting of a lazuli bunting with an indigo bunting on Fort Hood, Bell County. Bull. Texas Ornithol. Soc. 37 (1): 1–2.

Kraus, A., G. Guerra-Bautista, and D. Alarcón-Segovia. 1991. *Salmonella arizona* arthritis and septicemia associated with rattlesnake ingestion by patients with connective tissue diseases: A dangerous complication of folk medicine. J. Rheumatol. 18 (9): 1328–1331.

Kunath, C. E., and A. R. Smith, eds. 1968. The caves of the Stockton Plateau. Texas Speleol. Surv. 3 (2).

Lagesse, L. A., and N. B. Ford. 1996. Ontogenetic variation in the diet of the southern copperhead, *Agkistrodon contortrix*, in northeastern Texas. Texas J. Sci. 48 (1): 48–54.

Laughlin, H. E. 1966. A study of the interrelationships in natural populations of several species of lizards. PhD diss., Univ. of Texas.

Ledbetter, E. O., and A. E. Kutscher. 1969. The aerobic and anaerobic flora of rattlesnake fangs and venom. Arch. Environ. Health 19:770–778.

Lehmann, V. W. 1984. *Bobwhites in the Rio Grande plain of Texas.* College Station: Texas A&M Univ. Press.

Lewis, T. H. 1951. The biology of *Leiolopisma laterale* (Say). Amer. Midl. Nat. 45 (1): 232–240.

Lord, K. J. 1984. The zooarchaeology of Hinds Cave (41 VV 456). PhD diss., Univ. of Texas.

Loughry, W. J. 1987. The dynamics of snake harassment by black-tailed prairie dogs. Behaviour 103 (1–3): 27–48.

———. 1988. Population differences in how black-tailed prairie dogs deal with snakes. Behav. Ecol. Sociobiol. 22:61–67.

Lukowski, P. D. 1987. Archaeological investigations along the Leona River watershed, Uvalde County, Texas. Archaeological Survey Report 132. San Antonio: Univ. of Texas at San Antonio, Center for Archaeological Research.

Lundelius, E. L., Jr. 1985. Pleistocene vertebrates from Laubach Cave 1N. Austin Geol. Soc. Guidebook 8:41–45.

Lynott, M. J. 1980. Hypothesis testing and historic preservation at Bear Creek Shelter, Hill County, Texas. Bull. Texas Archaeol. Soc. 51:209–241.

Marmaduke, W. S. 1978. Prehistoric culture in Trans-Pecos Texas: An ecological explanation. PhD diss., Univ. of Texas.

Marr, J. C. 1944. Notes on amphibians and reptiles from the central United States. Amer. Midl. Nat. 32:478–490.

Martin, D. L. 2005. Diamondback: Enduring symbol of Texas. Rio Grande Valley Nature 3 (2): 9–12.

Martinez, R. R., J. C. Perez, E. E. Sanchez, and R. Campos. 1999. The antihemorrhagic factor of the Mexican ground squirrel, (*Spermophilus mexicanus*). Toxicon 37:949–954.

Masson, M. A. and M. W. Holderby. 1994. Subsistence patterns at 41HY209 and 41HY202: An analysis of vertebrate faunal remains. In *Archaic and Late Prehistoric human ecology in the Middle Onion Creek Valley, Hays County, Texas; Vol. 2: Topical Studies*, ed. R. A. Ricklis and M. B. Collins, 403–489. Studies in Archaeology 19. Austin: Univ. of Texas, Texas Archaeological Research Laboratory.

Maudlin, R. P., S. A. Tomka, and H. J. Shafer. 2004. *Millican Bench (41TV163), a multicomponent site in Travis County, Texas.* Archaeological Survey Report 351. San Antonio: Univ. of Texas at San Antonio, Center for Archaeological Research.

McAlister, W. H., and M. K. McAlister. 1993. *Matagorda Island: A naturalist's guide.* Austin: Univ. of Texas Press.

McClure, W. L. 1990. A snake "necklace" from the Morphiss Site. La Tierra 17 (1): 9–12.

McCrystal, H. K. 1991. The herpetofauna of the Big Bend region. Sonoran Herpetol. 4 (4): 137–141.

McCrystal, H. K., and R. J. Green. 1986. *Agkistrodon contortrix pictigaster* (Trans-Pecos copperhead) feeding. Herpetol. Rev. 17 (3): 61.

McDonald, J. 1974. Non-human bones from the Loeve-Fox sites: A preliminary analysis [Appendix II]. In *Archaeological investigations at the Loeve-Fox Site, Williamson County, Texas,* ed. E. R. Prewitt, 132–134. Research Report 49. Austin: Univ. of Texas, Texas Archaeological Survey.

McGregor, D. E., and J. E. Bruseth, eds. 1987. *Hunter-gatherer adaptations along the prairie margin: Site excavations and synthesis of prehistoric archaeology.* Richland Creek Technical Series 3. Dallas: Southern Methodist Univ., Institute for the Study of Earth and Man, Archaeological Research Program.

McGuff, P. and B. Davidson. 1978. Faunal data from sites excavated during the 1974 season at Palmetto Bend [Appendix II]. *In Prehistoric archaeological investigations at Palmetto Bend Reservoir: Phase 1, Jackson County, Texas,* ed. P. R. McGuff, 216–232. Survey Research Report 58. Austin: University of Texas, Texas Archaeological Survey.

McKeller, M. R., and J. C. Pérez. 2002. The effects of western diamondback rattlesnake (*Crotalus atrox*) venom on the production of antihemorrhagins and/or antibodies in the Virginia opossum (*Didelphis virginiana*). Toxicon 40:427–439.

McKinney, C. O., and R. E. Ballinger. 1966. Snake predators of lizards in western Texas. Southwest. Nat. 11:410–412.

McNease, L., and T. Joanen. 1977. Alligator diets in relation to marsh salinity. Proc. Ann. Conf. Southeast. Assoc. Fish Wildl. Agencies 31:36–40.

Mecham, J.S. 1958 [1959] Some Pleistocene amphibians and reptiles from Friesenhahn Cave, Texas. Southwest. Nat. 3:17–27.

Meinzer, W. 1993. *The Roadrunner.* Lubbock: Texas Tech Univ. Press.

Meissner, B.A. 1998. Vertebrate faunal remains. In *Mission San Jose Indian quarters wall base project, Bexar County, Texas,* ed. S. A. Tomka and A. A. Fox, 33–40. Archaeological Survey Report 278. San Antonio: Univ. of Texas at San Antonio, Center for Archaeological Research.

———. 1999. Analysis of vertebrate faunal remains from a Spanish colonial deposit at Mission San Antonio de Valero (the Alamo). Bull. Texas Archaeol. Soc. 70:281–313.

———. 1999. Vertebrate faunal remains. In *Archaeological investigations of rainwater catchment basins along the south wall of Mission San Jose, San Antonio Texas,* ed. S. A. Tomka and A. A. Fox, 39–46. Archaeological Survey Report 287.

San Antonio: Univ. of Texas at San Antonio, Center for Archaeological Research.

——. 2004. Analysis of vertebrate faunal remains. In *Excavations at the Alamo (41BX6) 1995 "Alamo Well" project*, ed. T. H. Guderjan, 37–56. San Antonio: St. Mary's Univ.

Menchaca, J. M., and J. C. Perez. 1981. The purification and characterization of an antihemorrhagic factor in opossum (*Didelphis virginiana*) serum. Toxicon 19:623–632.

Menger, R. 1905. Original observations, with photographic illustrations, on reptiles and insects of Texas. Bull. Sci. Soc. San Antonio 1 (1): 11–31.

——. 1913. *Texas nature observations and reminiscences*. San Antonio: Guessaz and Ferlet.

Milstead, W. W., J. S. Mecham, and H. McClintock. 1950. The amphibians and reptiles of the Stockton Plateau in northern Terrell County, Texas. Texas J. Sci. 2 (4): 543–562.

Minton, J. E. 1949. Coral snake preyed upon by the bullfrog. Copeia, 1949 (4): 288.

Minton, S. A., Jr. 1958 [1959]. Observations on amphibians and reptiles of the Big Bend region of Texas. Southwest. Nat. 3:28–54.

——. 1975. A note on the venom of an aged rattlesnake. Toxicon 13:73–74.

Minton, S. A., and S. A. Weinstein. 1986. Geographic and ontogenetic variation in venom of the western diamondback rattlesnake (*Crotalus atrox*). Toxicon 24 (1): 71–80.

Miranda, L., Jr., V. Mata-Silva, S. Dilks, H. Riveroll, Jr., and J. D. Johnson. 2008. *Crotalus molossus* (blacktail rattlesnake) morphology. Herpetol. Rev. 39 (1): 97.

Mitchell, J. D. 1903. The poisonous snakes of Texas, with notes on their habits. Trans. Texas Acad. Sci. 5 (2): 21–48.

Montgomery, W. B., and G. W. Schuett. 1989. Autumnal mating with subsequent production of offspring in the rattlesnake *Sistrurus miliarius streckeri*. Bull. Chicago Herpetol. Soc. 24 (11): 205–207.

Mueller, J. M., C. B. Dabbert, S. Demarais, and A. R. Forbes. 1999. Northern bobwhite chick mortality caused by red imported fire ants. J. Wildl. Manag. 63 (4): 1291–1298.

Murphy, R. W., and C. B. Crabtree. 1988. Genetic identification of a natural hybrid rattlesnake: *Crotalus scutulatus scutulatus* x *C. viridis viridis*. Herpetologica 44 (1): 119–123.

Murray, L. T. 1939. Annotated list of amphibians and reptiles from the Chisos Mountains. Contrib. Baylor Univ. Mus. 24:4–16.

Murray, P. R. 1987. Vertebrate faunal assemblage. In *The Bird Point Island and Adams Ranch sites: Methodological and theoretical contributions to north central Texas archaeology*, ed. J. E. Bruseth and W. A. Martin, 247–252. Richland Creek Technical Series 2. Dallas: Southern Methodist Univ., Archaeological Research Program.

Murry, P. A. 1978. Vertebrate faunal remains. In *Bear Creek shelter*, ed. M. J. Lynott, 48–70. Research Report 115. Dallas: Southern Methodist Univ., Archaeological Research Program.

———. 1982a. Prehistoric faunal ecology of the Lakeview Project: Phase two. In *Archaeological investigations at Lakeview Lake: 1979 and 1980*, ed. L. M. Raab, 247–255. Archaeological Monographs 2. Dallas: Southern Methodist Univ., Archaeological Research Program.

———. 1982b. Ecology, seasonality, and faunal utilization [Appendix a]. In *Settlement of the prairie margin: Archaeology of the Richland Creek Reservoir, Navarro and Freestone counties, Texas, 1980–1981; A research synopsis*, ed. L. M. Raab, 229–237. Dallas: Southern Methodist Univ., Department of Anthropology, Archaeological Research Program.

Noskin, G. A., and J. T. Clarke. 1990. *Salmonella arizonae* bacteremia as the presenting manifestation of human immunodeficiency virus infection following rattlesnake meat ingestion. Rev. Infect. Dis. 12 (3); 514–517.

Parmley, D. 1988. Holocene herpetofauna of Klein Cave, Kerr County, Texas. Southwest. Nat. 33 (3): 378–382.

Parrish, H. M. 1964. Texas snakebite statistics. Texas St. J. Med. 60:592–598.

Parrish, H. M., J. C. Goldner, and S. I. Silberg. 1966. Poisonous snake-bites causing no venenation. Postgrad. Med. 39 (3): 265–269.

Perez, J. C., W. C. Haws, V. E. Garcia, and B. M. Jennings, III. 1978. Resistance of warm-blooded animals to snake venoms. Toxicon 16 (4): 375–383.

Perez, J. C., W. C. Haws, and C. H. Hatch. 1978. Resistance of woodrats (*Neotoma micropus*) to *Crotalus atrox* venom. Toxicon 16:198–200.

Perez, J. C., S. Pichyangkul, and V. E. Garcia. 1979. The resistance of three species of warm-blooded animals to western diamondback rattlesnake (*Crotalus atrox*) venom. Toxicon 17:601–607.

Peter, D. E., and D. E. McGregor, eds. 1988. *Late Holocene prehistory of the Mountain Creek drainage*. Joe Pool Lake Archaeological Project, vol. 1. Dallas: Southern Methodist University, Archaeological Research Program.

Peterson, K. H. 1990. Conspecific and self-envenomation in snakes. Bull. Chicago Herpetol. Soc. 25:26–28.

Pichyangkul, S., and J. C. Perez. 1981. Purification and characterization of a naturally occurring antihemorrhagic factor in the serum of the hispid cotton rat (*Sigmodon hispidus*). Toxicon 19:205–215.

Pisani, G. R., and H. S. Fitch. 1992. A survey of Oklahoma's rattlesnake roundups. Kansas Herpetol. Soc. Newsl. 92:7–15.

Price, G. R. D. 1993. *Archaeological significance testing at sites 41MU60, 41MU61, 41MU62 and 41MU63, Montague County, Texas*. Austin: Texas Department of Transportation.

Quinn, H. R. 1979. Reproduction and growth of the Texas coral snake (*Micrurus fulvius tenere*). Copeia, 1979 (3): 453–463.

———. 1981. *Crotalus lepidus lepidus* (mottled rock rattlesnake) coloration. Herpetol. Rev. 12:79–80.

Quinn, J. R. 1985. Caspian terns respond to rattlesnake predation in a colony. Wilson Bull. 97 (2): 233–234.

Raun, G. G. 1959. Terrestrial and aquatic vertebrates of a moist, relict area in central Texas. Texas J. Sci. 11 (2): 158–171.

———. 1966. A population of woodrats (*Neotoma micropus*) in southern Texas. Texas Mem. Mus. Bull. 11:1–62.

Raun, G. G., and H. E. Laughlin. 1972. Sub-recent vertebrate remains from a site in southern Texas with comments on *Microtus* (*Pedomys*) *ludovicianus*. Southwest. Nat. 16:436–439.

Raun, G. G., and B. J. Wilks. 1964. Natural history of *Baiomys taylori* in southern Texas and competition with *Sigmodon hispidus* in a mixed population. Texas J. Sci. 16 (1): 28–49.

Rawn-Schatzinger, V. 1981. Faunal analysis [Appendix VII]. In *Cultural resources surveys and assessments in portions of Hidalgo and Willacy counties, Texas*, ed. W. D. Day, J. Laurens-Day, and E. R. Prewitt, 391–409. Austin: Prewitt and Associates.

Reams, R. D., C. J. Franklin, and J. M. Davis. 1999. *Micrurus fulvius tener* (Texas coral snake) diet. Herpetol. Rev. 30:228–229.

Reddell, J. R. 1970. A checklist of the cave fauna of Texas: VI. Additional records of vertebrates. Texas J. Sci. 22:139–158.

Reddell, J. R., and A. R. Smith, eds. 1965. The caves of Edwards County. Texas Speleol. Survey 2 (5–6).

Reynolds, R. P., and N. J. Scott, Jr. 1982. Use of a mammalian resource by a Chihuahuan snake community. In *Herpetological communities*, ed. N. J. Scott, Jr., 99–118. U.S. Dept. of the Interior, Fish and Wildlife Service.

Riley, K. B., D. Antoniskis, R. Maris, and J. M. Leedom. 1988. Rattlesnake capsule-associated *Salmonella arizona* infections. Arch. Intern. Med. 148:1207–1210.

Rogers, K. L. 1976. Herpetofauna of the Beck Ranch local fauna (Upper Pliocene: Blancan) of Texas. Publ. Mus. Michigan St. Univ. Paleontol. Ser. 1 (5): 163–200.

Rollins, D., and J. P. Carroll. 2001. Impacts of predation on northern bobwhite and scaled quail. Wildl. Soc. Bull. 29 (1): 39–51.

Roth, E. D., and J. A. Johnson. 2004. Size-based variation in antipredator behavior within a snake (*Agkistrodon piscivorus*) population. Behav. Ecol. 15 (2): 365–370.

Rudolph, D. C., and S. J. Burgdorf. 1997. Timber rattlesnakes and Louisiana pine snakes of the west Gulf Coastal Plain: Hypotheses of decline. Texas J. Sci. 49 (3) Suppl.: 111–122.

Ruick, J. D., Jr. 1948. Collecting coral snakes, *Micrurus fulvius tenere*, in Texas. Herpetologica 4:215–216.

Runkles, F. A. 1964. The Garza site: A neo-American campsite near Post, Texas. Bull. Texas Archaeol. Soc. 35:101–125.

Russell, F. E. 1983. *Snake venom poisoning*. Great Neck, N.Y.: Scholium International.

Sabath, M. and R. Worthington. 1959. Eggs and young of certain Texas reptiles. Herpetologica 15 (1): 31–32.

Sagebiel, J. C. 1998. Late Pleistocene fauna and environment at Zesch Cave, Mason County, Texas. MS thesis, Univ. of Texas.

Salazar, J. D., and C. S. Lieb. n.d. Geographic diet variation of Mojave rattlesnake. Manuscript on file, Museum of Arid Lands Biology, Univ. Texas at El Paso.

Schad, G. A. 1962. Studies on the genus *Kalicephalus* (Nematoda: Diaphanocephalidae) II: A taxonomic revision of the genus *Kalicephalus* Molin, 1861. Can. J. Zool. 40:1035–1165.

Schmidly, D. J. 1983. *Texas mammals east of the Balcones Fault zone*. College Station: Texas A&M Univ. Press.

Schmidt, K. P. 1945. The girl who had never been bitten by a rattlesnake: A Texas folktale. Chicago Nat. 8 (2): 30–31.

Schmidt, K. P., and T. F. Smith. 1944. Amphibians and reptiles of the Big Bend region of Texas. Field Mus. Nat. Hist. Zool. Ser. 29 (5): 75–96.

Schuett, G. W. and J. C. Gillingham. 1986. Sperm storage and multiple paternity in the copperhead, *Agkistrodon contortrix*. Copeia, 1986 (3): 807–811.

Schwenk, K. 1995. The serpent's tongue. Nat. Hist. 104 (4): 48–54.

Seifert, W. 1972. Amphibians and reptiles in Texas, Part two: Habitat, variations and intergradations of the Trans-Pecos copperhead *Agkistrodon contortrix pictigaster* in Texas. Bull. Dallas Mus. Nat. Hist. 2:1–10.

Sheridan, B. S., G. R. Wilson, and P. J. Weldon. 1989. Aerobic bacteria from the skin of the rattlesnake, *Crotalus atrox*. J. Herpetol. 23 (2): 200–202.

Sherrod, C. L. 2004. Coral snake eats ribbon snake. in litt., 041110 (*Micrurus fulvius*).

Silvy, N. J., D. Rollins, and S. W. Whisenant. 2007. Scaled quail ecology and life history. In *Texas quails: Ecology and management*, ed. L. A. Brennan, 65–88. College Station: Texas A&M Univ. Press.

Simpich, F. 1928. So big Texas. Natl. Geogr. Mag. 53 (6): 637–693.

Sinclair, T. 2007. Coral snake eats broad-headed skink. in litt., 071105 (*Micrurus fulvius*).

Skinner, S. A. 1979. The bushwack shelter (X41 KR 116), Kerr County, Texas. J. So. Texas Archaeol. Assoc. 6 (2): 3–12.

Slaughter, B. H., and W. L. McClure. 1965. The Sims Bayou local fauna: Pleistocene of Houston, Texas. Texas J. Sci. 17 (4): 404–417.

Sloan, D. L. 1987. Northern bobwhite nesting, activity patterns and habitat use in two grazing systems in the Texas Coastal Bend. MS thesis, Stephen F. Austin State Univ.

Smith, A. R., and J. R. Reddell, eds. 1971. The caves of Kimble County. Texas Speleol. Surv. 3 (6).

Smith, D. D., N. A. Laposha, R. Powell, and J. S. Parmerlee, Jr. 1985. *Crotalus molossus* (blacktail rattlesnake) anomaly. Herpetol. Rev. 16:78–79.

Spencer, C. L. 2003. Geographic variation in the morphology, diet and reproduction of a widespread pitviper, the western diamondback rattlesnake (*Crotalus atrox*). PhD diss., Univ. of Texas at Arlington.

Steele, D. G. 1986a. Analysis of faunal remains. In *The Clemente and Herminia Hinojosa site, 41 JW 8: A Toyah horizon campsite in southern Texas*, ed. S. L. Black, 108–136. San Antonio: Univ. of Texas at San Antonio, Center for Archaeological Research.

———. 1986b. Analysis of vertebrate faunal remains from 41 LK 201, Live Oak County, Texas. In *Archaeological investigations at 41 LK 201, Choke Canyon Reservoir, southern Texas*, ed. C. L. Highley, 200–249. Choke Canyon Series 11. San Antonio: Univ. of Texas at San Antonio, Center for Archaeological Research.

Steele, D. G., and Hunter, C. A. 1986. Analysis of vertebrate faunal remains from 41 MC 222 and 41 MC 296, McMullen County, Texas. In *The prehistoric sites at Choke Canyon Reservoir, southern Texas: Results of phase II archaeological investigations*, ed. G. D. Hall, T. R. Hester, and S. L. Black, 452–502. San Antonio: Univ. of Texas at San Antonio, Center for Archaeological Research.

Steele, D. G., and E. R. Mokry, Jr. 1985. Archaeological investigations of seven prehistoric sites along Oso Creek, Nueces County, Texas. Bull. Texas Archaeol. Soc. 54:288–308.

Stevenson, J. O., and L. H. Meitzen. 1946. Behavior and food habits of Sennett's white-tailed hawk in Texas. Wilson Bull. 58:198–205.

Stewart, B. G. 1984. *Agkistrodon contortrix laticinctus* (broad-banded copperhead) combat. Herpetol. Rev. 15 (1): 17.

Stinnett, J. K. 1975. The terrestrial vertebrates of the Devil's Sinkhole–Hackberry Creek area. In *Devil's Sinkhole area--headwaters of the Nueces River: A natural area survey*, ed. D. Kennard, 75–81. Austin: University of Texas.

Straight, R., J. L. Glenn, and C. C. Snyder. 1976. Antivenom activity of rattlesnake blood plasma. Nature 261:259-260.

Strasser, F. D. 1931. An encounter between a collared lizard and a rattlesnake. Bull. Antivenin Inst. Amer. 5 (2): 41.

Strecker, J. K., Jr. 1908. The reptiles and batrachians of McLennan County, Texas. Proc. Biol. Soc. Wash. 21:69–84

———. 1927. Chapters from the life-histories of Texas reptiles and amphibians: Part two. Contrib. Baylor Univ. Mus. 10:1–14.

———. 1935a. Albino snakes. In Notes on the zoology of Texas from the unpublished manuscripts of John Kern Strecker, ed. W. J. Williams, 29. Baylor Bull. 38 (3).

———. 1935b. Notes on the pit-vipers in McLennan County, Texas. In Notes on the zoology of Texas from the unpublished manuscripts of John Kern Strecker, ed. W. J. Williams, 26–28. Baylor Bull. 38 (3).

Strecker, J. K., and W. J. Williams. 1928. Field notes on the herpetology of Bowie County, Texas. Contrib. Baylor Univ. Mus. 17:1–19.

Svihla, A. 1931. Life history of the Texas rice rat (*Oryzomys palustris texensis*). J. Mamm. 12 (3): 238–242.

Swannack, T. M., and M. R. J. Forstner. 2003. *Micrurus fulvius tener* (Texas coral snake) diet. Herpetol. Rev. 34 (4): 376.

Taylor, A. J. 1995. Summary and consideration of cultural features. In vol. 1 of *Archeological investigations at the Loma Sandia site (41LK28): A prehistoric cemetery and campsite in Live Oak County, Texas*, ed. A. J. Taylor and C. L. Highley, 359–404. Studies in Archaeology 20. Austin: Univ. of Texas, Texas Archaeological Research Laboratory.

Taylor, W. P. 1953a. Food habits of the gray fox (*Urocyon cinereoargenteus*) in the Edwards Plateau, Texas. Austin: Texas Game and Fish Commission.

———. 1953b. Food habits of the opossum in the Edwards Plateau, Texas. Austin: Texas Game and Fish Commission.

———. 1953c. Food habits of the raccoon in Central Texas. Austin: Texas Game and Fish Commission.

———. 1954. Food habits and notes on life history of the ring-tailed cat in Texas. J. Mamm. 35 (1): 55–63.

Tennant, A. 1984. *The snakes of Texas*. Austin: Texas Monthly Press, Austin.

Theakston, R. D. G., and H. A. Reid. 1978. Changes in the biological properties of venom from *Crotalus atrox* with ageing. Period. Biol. 80 (suppl. 1): 123–133.

Thomas, R. G., and F. H. Pough. 1979. The effect of rattlesnake venom on digestion of prey. Toxicon 17 (3): 221–228.

Thornton, O. W., Jr., and J. R. Smith. 1995. Late prehistoric snakes of E. V. Spence and O. H. Ivie Reservoir basins of Coke, Coleman, Concho, and Runnels counties, Texas. Texas J. Sci. 47 (4): 295–307.

Tinkle, D. W. 1962. Reproductive potential and cycles in female *Crotalus atrox* from northwestern Texas. Copeia, 1962 (2): 306–313.

———. 1967. The life and demography of the side-blotched lizard, *Uta stansburiana*. Misc. Publ. Mus. Zool. Univ. Michigan 132:1–182.

Trauth, S. E., and C. T. McAllister. 1995. Vertebrate prey of selected Arkansas snakes. Proc. Arkansas Acad. Sci. 49:188–192.

Tu, A. T. 1982. Chemistry of rattlesnake venoms. In *Rattlesnake venoms: Their actions and treatment*, ed. A. T. Tu, 247–312. New York: Dekker.

Turpin, S. A., and M. W. Davis. 1990. *The 1989 TAS field school: Devils River State Natural Area*. Bull. Texas Archaeol. Soc. 61:1–58.

Urabek, R. L. 1989. Evaluation of predator guards for black-bellied whistling duck nest-boxes. Great Plains Wildl. Damage Contr. Wkshp. Proc., 1989: 144–147.

Van Devender, T. R., and G. L. Bradley. 1994. Late Quaternary amphibians and reptiles from Maravillas Canyon Cave, Texas, with discussion of the biogeography and evolution of the Chihuahuan Desert herpetofauna. In *Herpetology of the North American deserts: Proceedings of a symposium*, ed. P. R. Brown and J. W. Wright, 23–53. Van Nuys, Calif: Southwestern Herpetologists Society.

Vincent, J. W. 1982. Color pattern variation in *Crotalus lepidus lepidus* (Viperidae) in southwestern Texas. Southwest. Nat. 27 (3): 263–272.

Voss, W. J. 1961. A survey of ixodorhynchid mites on snakes. MS thesis, Texas Tech. Univ.

Watson, R. P. 1982. The archaeology of Aquilla Reservoir: Implications for a regional research design for the central Brazos River basin, Texas. PhD diss., Univ. of Texas.

Webber, J. J. Z., J. M. Compton, and E. J. Reitz. 2002. Artifacts: Section E: Faunal [Chapter 9]. In *Archaeological investigations at the last Spanish colonial mission established on the Texas frontier: Nuestra Señora del Refugio (41RF1), Refugio County, Texas*. Vol. 1: *Archaeological investigations*, ed. C. L. Tennis, 271–311. Report 39. Austin: Texas Department of Transportation, Environmental Affairs Division, Archaeological Studies Program; and Archaeological Survey Report 315. San Antonio: Univ. of Texas at San Antonio, Center for Archaeological Research.

Weir, J. 1992. The Sweetwater rattlesnake round-up: A case study in environmental ethics. Conserv. Biol. 6 (1): 116–127.

Weissenberg, S., M. Ovadia, G. Fleminger, and E. Kochva. 1991. Antihemorrhagic factors from the blood serum of the western diamondback rattlesnake *Crotalus atrox*. Toxicon 29:807–818.

Werler, J. E., and J. R. Dixon. 2000. *Texas snakes: Identification, distribution, and natural history*. Austin: Univ. of Texas Press.

Whitson, M. A. 1983. The roadrunner: Clown of the desert. Natl. Geogr. Mag. 163 (5): 694–702.

Wilson, S. C. 1954. Snake fight. Texas Game Fish Mag. 12 (5): 16–17.

Wingert, W. A., and J. Wainschel. 1975. Diagnosis and management of envenomation by poisonous snakes. South. Med. J. 68 (8): 1015–1026.

Womochel, D. R. 1977. Taphonomy and paleoecology of the Slaton local fauna (Pleistocene, Texas). PhD diss., Texas Tech Univ.

Wood, J. E. 1954. Food habits of furbearers of the upland post oak region of Texas. J. Mamm. 35:406–415.

Wright, J. F. 1997. The Asa Warner site (41ML46), McLennan County, Texas. Bull. Texas Archaeol. Soc. 68:215–261.

Wylie, S.R. 1974. A comparison of the ecological niches of coachwhips, *Masticophis flagellum* (Shaw), and racers, *Coluber constrictor* Linnaeus, in Texas. MS thesis, Univ. of Texas at Arlington.

Yancey, F. D., II, W. Meinzer, and C. Jones. 1997. Aberrant morphology in western diamondback rattlesnakes (*Crotalus atrox*). Occ. Pap. Mus. Texas Tech Univ. 164:1–4.

Zamudio, K. R., D. L. Hardy, Sr., M. Martins, and H. W. Greene. 2000. Fang tip spread, puncture distance, and suction for snake bite. Toxicon 38:723–728.

Zepeda, H., E. D. Rael, and R. A. Knight. 1985. Isolation of two phospholipases A$_2$ from Mojave rattlesnake (*Crotalus scutulatus scutulatus*) venom and variation of immunologically related venom properties in different populations. Comp. Biochem. Physiol. 81B (2): 319–324.

INDEX

Frithjof Schuon

ROAD TO THE HEART

POEMS

Library of Congress Cataloging-in-Publication Data
Schuon, Frithjof, 1907-
    Road to the heart: poems / by Frithjof Schuon.
        p. cm.
    ISBN 0-941532-20-8 : $10.00
    1. Religious poetry.   I. Title.
PR9105.5.S38   1995
821'.914—dc20

For information address World Wisdom Books, Inc.
P.O. Box 2682, Bloomington, Indiana 47402-2682

ROAD TO THE HEART

I

THE GARLAND

THE RIVER

Without beginning is the river's start:
It rises from the mountain's unknown ground
And seeks the endless. So the wise man's heart:
The river flows; its end is never found.

Neither the mountain nor the sea can limit
The river's song. Love flows from God to God;
Forms have an end, yet timeless is the Spirit.

CREATION

They think that out of nothing God has made
The Universe, and that it is His shade —
Less than reality, more than a play.
The world is real and unreal, so to say.

The hidden Treasure never had been shown;
God made the world, He wanted to be known.

THE MYSTERY

Some people ask: Had God to make the world?
First let us say: there is in God no need;
And then: He radiates His nature's Good;
And so He did conceive the cosmic seed.

We should say that Reality is He
Who needs no thing; but Māyā wants to be.

THE GOOD

Why should the Sovereign Good not overflow?
Its brightness and its bliss cannot but glow.
A hidden treasure nobody can see;
Therefore the whole creation had to be.

We have been made in order that we might
Be as a mirror for the Godhead's Light.

REMEMBER

O men of little faith, do not forget
What prophets, saints and pious men have said:
Remember God, God will remember you.
A better thing on earth we cannot do.

Albeit low, we should not be ashamed;
God wanted us; He needed to be named.

REGINA COELI

Thou art more than a symbol; Thou art near
To me as blood and heart; Thou art the air
That makes me live, that makes me pure and wise;
A sweet and tender air from Paradise.

Thou art more than the words describing Thee
And more than all the sacred songs that we
Sing in Thy praise; my ecstasy was Thine
Before God's very making of the vine.

THE DRINK

Because the drink is of an earthly brand
The drinker's heart they do not understand.
Now earthly beauty, to the wise, is more
Than just a sign; it is an open door.

They think the lover's pilgrimage will fail
Because he meets not Laylā, but her veil.
They do not see that with the Angel's kiss
We drink the wine of everlasting Bliss.

IMMANENCE

They think the world is blooming, while the heart
Renouncing it for God is poor and dark;
In this abyss, they say, thou wilt not find
The golden Paradise thou hast in mind;
They see not that the mystery of night
Means Laylā dancing in a globe of light.

Thy deepest heart contains the holy shrine,
The naked goddess and the cup of wine.

LAYLĀ

She may be dark, a deep and silent night,
Yet she is beautiful, a wondrous sight.
By greedy men she never will be seen;
Her peerless body hides behind a screen.

Her breasts are like the sun, now East, now West;
They are the pilgrim's refuge and his rest;
She gives him joy and peace with tender lips
And with the rapture of her dancing hips.

MEMENTO

Thou knowest that thou canst not change the world;
Renounce it, let things be what they must be.
There are things we can change and others not;
There is a meaning in all destiny.

Do not forget: there is a Sovereign Good
Whose Mercy may defeat Fatality.
The reason is that Being's deepest sound
Comes from the harp of pure Felicity.

THE WAVE

There are things we can change and others not:
Let us accept what is our written fate.
In God's Compassion we will find no spot;
And we should know that Being's inmost sound
Is sheer Beatitude. And faith will wait;
For faith means patience. Happy is the man
Who Mercy's Mystery and Way has found —

Who with his love and in his very core
Becomes a Wave that leads to Allah's Shore.

MĀYĀ

The Sovereign Good is real, the world is dream;
The dream-world has its roots in the Supreme,
Who casts His image in the endless sea
Of things that may be or that may not be.

The fabric of the Universe is made
Of rays and circles, or of light and shade;
It veils from us the Power's burning Face
And unveils Beauty and Its saving Grace.

TIME

Even the wisest cannot change the Law
Of stern and merciless Necessity
That rules the world. Life is a measured dream;
Time is a night of cold Eternity.

"I may be black yet I am beautiful":
Within the Law is Love and Liberty
And saving Grace. For Being's very heart
Is Joy, and Peace, and Immortality.

THE ISLAND

Islands of bliss and everlasting youth,
Floating like flowers on an endless sea
And never touched by sorrows from this world:
Such happy islands thou wilt never see.

Behold: what thou hast dreamt of may be real,
It is not elsewhere, it is what thou art
If thou rememb'rest God; then thou wilt find
The golden island in thy deepest heart.

The singing of a flute came from the sea;
The waters vanished, and the flute was me.

NEARNESS

As long as we are clad with time and space,
Men think, we will not reach the Heavens' place;
In exile here we scarcely can rejoice
In God, because so feeble is. our voice.

To saving Truth they give not willing ear:
With God in mind His Paradise is near.
And "if there is a Paradise on earth" —
An old inscription tells us — "it is here."

It was meant for the palace of a king.
We mean God's Name; so let us dance and sing!

THE NAME

Thy Name is wine and honey, melody
That shapes our sacred way and destiny.
Who is the Speaker and who is the Word?
Where is the song Eternity has heard?

The liberating Word comes from the sky
Of Grace and Mercy; and we wonder why
Such gift can be; the truth is not so far:
Thy Name is That which is, and what we are.

THE SYMBOL

The Symbol thou shouldst carry in thy heart,
And in the Symbol thou shouldst always dwell;
It is a treasure and a shelter, and
A weapon and a saving boat as well.

It is a divine Grace which gives us life;
Within this saving Grace thou canst not fall.
And know: thou also art the Symbol and
The Sign of God, or thou art not at all.

FREEDOM

Thou feelest that this earthly world is sad,
But o'er this sadness thou shouldst not lament;
Do not say that the Universe is bad.

For every earthly shadow has an end,
And endless is the hidden bliss in things;
Life may be heavy, but the soul has wings.

The double nature of this world behold:
One side is iron, and the other gold.
Thy blissful inner nature thou shouldst see,
Then thou wilt know: God made it pure and free.

THE SPOT

The world is woven of Necessity
And Play: this web is cosmic Harmony.
Don't think the world is like a wicked plot,
But know that evil is a fading spot.

Even this single spot will disappear,
It is an instant in a blessèd year.
It had to be, but do not wonder why;
The Possible is endless like the sky.

We have to travel through this earthly shade;
Yet for the Light of Heaven we are made.

WORLD'S WEB

Mysterious is World's hidden harmony;
The Universe is like a web of dreams
Which come and go — haphazard, as it seems —

Like in the wind a passing melody.
The wisest cannot change the play of things;
But he is rooted in Eternity —

In a Beatitude that flows and sings.

LALLĀ

Shrī Lallā Yogīshwarī had to enter
From Māyā's reign into her deepest center.
"And therefore naked I began to dance";
Shrī Lakshmī cast on her a blessing glance.

Body and heart: give each of them its due.
For "Beauty is the splendor of the True".

HAQĪQAH

Form can be true, but Truth is never form;
Haqīqah dances with her thousand veils —
Protecting thus the ignorant from harm —
Yet to the wise her Beauty She reveals.

And Beauty's nature is to liberate.
The secret Grace is "Night", because the day
May mean world's din. Impersonal is Truth;
But sweet and loving is Haqīqah's Ray.

24

TRUTH

"In Beauty is the splendor of the True":
  If Truth we know, we will know Beauty too.
  And if in Beauty we can see the Good,
  Our spirit understands all that it should.

  Words in our earthly language may be weak,
  Yet Truth is strong; with Heaven's Heart we speak
  To show a path to living's inmost duty.

"Allah is beautiful and He loves Beauty":
  There is a Splendor we can hear and see;
  A mirror of the True we ought to be.

JAMĀL

Beauty is ours if we belong to God;
From outside let it stream into the heart.
What comes from God must lead us back to Him;
The beautiful is not of worldly art.

If you see Truth in Beauty, all is well;
Unselfish is the love that makes us wise.
To see the pleasure only, leads to hell;
Love God, then Beauty leads to Paradise.

The earthly good reveals the Good as such;
First see the Essence, and the form will shine.
In love of Truth there is a hidden death;
So die in God before you drink the wine.

CONFESSION

She, my Belovèd, is a wondrous day;
And I, who love Her, I am life and death
And storm and lightning, and my word is wine;
The world lies in my blood and in my breath.

O thou who seekest me, do never ask
Which is my homeland, nor what is my name;
The Universe is made of Light and Love,
And from this Light and from this Love I came.

ONE WORD

There is one Word, it is the saving key:
Dwell thou in God, and God will dwell in thee.
Out of compassion to our world He came;
His are two homes on earth: our heart, His Name.

THE CHOICE

Life is a choice: to love or not to love
What makes us live, the Sovereign Good above
This petty world; to love what makes us free
From nothingness; to be or not to be.

CONCLUSION

This Garland comes from Heaven, and I pray
To Heaven it may trace a golden Way.
It must be so; for what comes from Above
By itself brings us back to Light and Love.

Limited are the words, not what is meant;
For neither Truth nor Beauty has an end.

II

ANSWERS

KNOWLEDGE

There are things we do know and others not;
Knowledge of space and time I do not miss.
Maybe I do not know what people are
Or what I am; I know that Being is.

SCIENCE

Some say the Universe is like a book
And at the stars for Knowledge we should look.
Whatever brain and heart may understand —
With patient faith we are in Heaven's Hand.

THE FENCE

What is the magic of this World? A fence
Around That which to being gives a sense.
To draw us downwards heaviness will try;
Truth brings us to the endless open Sky.

QUESTIONS

There are things our poor thinking cannot find;
Infinity of space it can't discern.
So we may ask: what is this useless mind?
What are its objects, what is brain's concern?

The wise sees with the Heart's immortal face,
His mind is never troubled by the mask
Of Māyā. What is endless? what is space?
All is a proof of God — so do not ask.

ENIGMA

Infinity of number, space and time
And possibility is an abyss
For human brains; they find in it no rhyme.
Yet it proves God; it shows what Being is.

If there were not the Real above the mist
Of Māyā, space and time could not exist.

GNOSIS

On one side, there is consciousness, that knows,
And on the other side, there is the known;
Whereas in God, in His most Holy Name,
Knowing and Being ever are the same.

And so it is with Love: the "Thou and I";
For in each other's life they want to die;
From East to West Love brings the mighty Sun.
The Lover and the Loved: they will be One.

*If you wish to receive a copy
of the latest World Wisdom Books brochure
and to be placed on our mailing list
please send us this card.*

PLEASE PRINT

Book in which this card was found _____

NAME _____

ADDRESS _____

CITY & STATE _____

ZIP OR POSTAL CODE _____   COUNTRY _____
                                          (IF OUTSIDE U.S.A.)

WORLD WISDOM BOOKS, INC.

Mailing List
P.O. Box 2682
Bloomington, IN 47402-2682

THE PLAY

There is no melody without a truth;
There is no truth without a melody.
The very Universe is like a book.
Combining sternest facts with poetry;
If to our mind a lofty truth is clear,
The music of its evidence we hear.

And if on destiny we cast a look:
Without God's Mercy, Justice cannot be.
To Harmony Existence always tends;
Its play of laws and graces never ends.

Sometimes life gives us more and sometimes less;
Our substance is pure Being's Happiness.

COSMOS

Cosmic infinity is not the same
As God's Infinity; it must be round
— A sphere that out of God's own Radiance came —
Because by cosmic limits it is bound.

The two Realities we could compare:
A perfect ball within the endless air.
Perfection is Creation's wondrous root;
Infinity: Life of the Absolute.

VEDĀNTA

Brahma and Māyā: this has been revealed.
Māyā in Brahma: for He was concealed
And in His Silence He became the Word.
Māyā alone? This never has been heard.

Brahma in Māyā: for the Most-High can
Reveal His Grace in Angel and in Man.

Brahma alone: "I am That which I am";
First Silence, then the Word.
Brahma Satyam.

THE WAY

Within our deepest center dwells the Self;
And so they say: you ought to realize
Your own divinity. But they forget:
Without God's help we never can be wise.
Ignoring this, too many go astray.

With Heaven's Grace alone we find the Way.

DREAMING

Some people teach: dream is reality,
Reality is dream; priority
Can be ascribed to either. In this case
A dreaming dog could have a wise man's place

Real is the wise man's wisdom, not his state,
Whatever in a dream may be his fate.
The whole World is a dream with dreams; but he
Who dreams is all: it is the cosmic "We".

INQUIRY

"Ask who thou art, and thou wilt find the Self."
   The sense is true, the wording is too bold.
   For your inquiry you need Heaven's help;
   Without God's Grace the thought is dry and cold.

   You heard part of the Truth, you need the whole
   Reality: with God you reach the Goal.

THE OFFERING

The calling of God's Name, some people think,
Is easy, there must be a missing link.
Now with all that we are it must be done,
For otherwise its saving bliss is gone.

You offer it to God? Then understand:
Give with the heart, not only with the hand.
You call your Lord and then you pray with hope;
To Heaven this will be the saving rope.

FEAR

Some dreamers think: if you love God, then all
Is well. But they forget: not any call
To God will He accept; you are a fool
If you ignore that Love requires Rule.

For in the mystery of Love is Fear;
Through pious distance only you come near.

THE POINT

A mystic said: God is a playful child,
He makes fruits sweet and bitter, hot and mild.
Now God is limitless — this point is missed —
So He permits the "nothing" to exist.

Explaining God, you should not simplify;
The Possible is vast, you don't know why.
The naught wears being's dress; it is World's fate.
Absurdity must be; and God is great!

DISCERNMENT

Nothing on earth is bad — some people muse —
Except the "I", the "mine". There is a link
Cruelly missing; see things as they are!
Virtue is not forgetting how to think.

For God nothing is bad, these people mean;
He manifests Himself, and all is clean;
All is His trace, except the "I", the "mine";
And upon all the rest the sun will shine!
They overlook the question's very clue:
If all is good, then "mine" is perfect too.

Read in the Psalms; King David never would
Have said that all his enemies were good.
God is in our existence and our powers,
Not in Good's absence. Blessèd be His flowers!

TRANSCENDENCE

Philosophers may say: God is above
Both good and evil, white and black — one should
Know that He is transcendent. They forget:
Transcendence is Itself the Sovereign Good.

There is an opposition: wrong and right;
Do not forget that white alone is white!
Good is not good because we know the bad,
But through the Bliss its very Substance had.

Before the World emerged from Being's Might.

GREATNESS

You ask me what is greatness: it is not
A quality of man; it comes from God.
Our heart must know before it is too late:
Only our consciousness of God is great.

There is one consciousness of Him, not two;
A thousand mirrors drink the single Light.
Contingency is dream, but Truth is right;
Be what thou art and ask not who is who.

III

VIRGIN NATURE

VIRGIN NATURE

Although man always king on Earth has been,
Creation is his mother and a queen.
So take your living from this earthly place,
Not with a foolish pride, but saying grace.

You fear the Lord: respect His holy shade.
You love the Maker: love the work He made.
And let the hunter for his victim pray;
Its Archetype has given it, they say.

SPACE

The North, the South; the East and then the West:
Their mysteries we carry in our breast.
Zenith, Nadir, Spirit and Earth, 'tis we:
Purity, Love, Strength and Serenity.

Each value in the universal frame
Within our soul and spirit is the same.
Each quarter or each quality of Space
Shows a divine and cosmic Beauty's face.

So let us hear Eternal Wisdom's call:
Be thyself truly, and thou art the All.

TELL ME

Tell me why thou hast loved the mountain top,
Its serene silence and its purity,
And I will tell thee that our spirit's rest
Is solitude with God; serenity
Above the noise of thoughts. And tell me why
Thou lov'st the secret of the whispering wood,
Its sacredness and dark security,
And I will tell thee that our lasting joy
Is union, love within our deepest heart,
Diving into our being's Mystery;
Union with what I am, and what thou art.

PTE-SAN-WIN

She came, a holy maiden clad with air
And walking as a deer, with playful hair
And blissful breasts; she brought a wondrous good,
A living prayer fashioned of stone and wood.

Maybe the Sacred Pipe we could compare
To Krishna's Flute, which gave us Heaven's food:
Half a command to make us wise and strong
And half a joy, a liberating song.

She was a snow-white calf, and then a girl
Naked as truth and spotless as a pearl.
Down from the Sky she brought the Praying Pipe;
And she will come again, when time is ripe.

STRAIGHTNESS

In presence of the Pipe, they did not lie;
The sacred Smoke brought prayers up to the Sky.
Within the Sacred, life is pure and straight;
Drinking the Light, man's heart will radiate.

DANCE

The magic power of a sacred song,
The thunder of a drum afar one hears.
The movement of the stars is in the dance,
The everlasting music of the spheres.

Our inner truth needs to be heard and seen:
The dance means our deep nature and its speech.
Our body shows the language of the Self;
It lets us grasp what thinking cannot reach.

Dancing is born of nature's inner part;
From thence it comes, then goes back to the Heart.

WÁMBALI GALESHKA

He is the Lightning and the golden Ray
Which from the Sun comes downwards to the land
Of human joy and pain, the ancients say.

The Spotted Eagle carries us away
From Earth to Heaven, as God's saving Hand;
Blessèd the man who is the Angel's prey!

HEART'S WISDOM

It was within yourself, what Heaven brought.
What comes from God is in your heart the wine
Of Bliss and Wisdom. It will ne'er be found
By those who do not stand on sacred ground.

The singing of a flute came from Above;
The flute was in my heart; the song was Love.
It was the Ocean's endless melody:
A song of God and of Eternity.

PRAYER

"Grandfather, hear my words, I talk to Thee:
Look down, take pity, not alone on me
But on my people," prays a noble mind.
In this a deeper meaning thou wilt find.

When thou invokest God, His Grace is thine,
But like the living sunlight it will shine
For others too; the sacred, saving Sound
Will bless believing people all around.

A Sound that always in our heart should be;
A Wave of Bliss, Peace, Immortality.

IV

CREATURES

ANGEL

Created are the Angels, yet divine;
To that their glorious power is the clue.
Man is ambiguous, what can we say?
Potentially he is an Angel too.

ANIMALS

Most animals are horizontal, since
Their homeland is not other than this Earth;
But man's essential stance is vertical;
Free will to choose Salvation proves his worth.
Nobility some animals possess:
The genius of their symbol lives in them.
They can be more than a corrupted man;
Only their possibilities are less.

Be humble when you meet creation, for
An animal may be a sacred door.
Do not despise a noble plant, a stone:
They bring a message from God's blessèd Throne.

DIMENSIONS

The Eagle with the lightning shares his flight;
Among the water lilies swims the Swan.
With thunderstorm comes Revelation's Light;
Calm is the heart who with the Ray is one.

The two dimensions make the wise man's soul;
Wisdom is not a part, it is the whole.

IMAGE

The buffalo, the deer: with priestly horns
And antlers, and with strength and majesty,
They mean both Earth and Heaven. So we might
Combine the root and crown in harmony;

With depth and height Heart's image will be right.

LEVELS

The lion's wrath goes with serenity;
Yet his celestial model needs no fight.
For the Eternal Sun means Strength and Peace:
The burning Rigor goes with blissful Light.

On Earth, hard oppositions must appear
Even within the good, for World is dark;
Disharmony is earthly level's mark;
Empyrean's Law is Peace; for God is near.

MAN

Man on this earth is Heaven's incarnation;
His nature he forgot and his vocation.
He should remember with a pious awe:
His very substance is a sacred Law —

A Law involving work and dignity,
Faith in a destiny he cannot see.
Happy the man who without sight believes —
Who feeling death and Immortality
To God his life, his heart, his being gives.

ARCHETYPES

The blessèd Angels are the archetypes
Of man's most noble possibilities;
The archetypes of Angels are in God,
In all His Qualities and Mysteries,
Immeasurable the Empyrean's road.

And then: our archetype is also that
Which we will be in Heaven. Ask not where
We came from; in the Godhead is our home.
Look at the Sky. Our roots were always there.

V

ROAD TO THE HEART

THE SONG

A finite image of Infinity:
This is the purpose of all poetry.
All human work to its last limits tends;
Its Archetype in Heaven never ends.
What is the sense of Beauty and of Art?
To show the way into our inmost Heart —

To listen to the music of the Sky;
And then to realize: the Song was I.

GRATITUDE

Ungrateful are those on this earthly road
Who do complain that life is made of tears,
That happiness on earth one cannot find,
That we are made of sorrows and of fears.

Our soul itself is what we seek and need:
Our very heart is a relieving shade
And at the rim of night a rising sun.
Of Heaven's Peace and Joy our souls are made.

PRUDENCE

There is the faith of simple people, and
There is deep Wisdom on the other hand;
Don't think there is a problem after death;
There is no scission in Salvation's land.

Don't say thou seekest God, not Paradise,
That for created things thou art too wise.
On earth to Heaven's Way we give its due;
In Heaven God knows best what He will do.

INTENTION

Don't turn to God for favors in the Way;
Remembrance by itself is happiness.
A mere desire brings no inwardness;
Be happy then, and pray because you pray.

THE PATH

There are the servants of the Sovereign Good;
There are the seekers of the Inner Sun.
There are two manners of approaching God
The Most High; yet the twofold Path is one.

SINCERITY

Prayer is more than just an easy fact,
Because with all our being we then act.

Sense of the true, peace, generosity:
Each virtue is our being's golden key.

"Thou art all-beautiful, there is no spot
In thee"; our soul is pure, or we are not.

THE REAL

Among our aspirations, one comes first:
It is our longing for the Real; our thirst
For rays of Everlasting Truth that brings
Us what we need above all worldly things.

Two main dimensions has the human soul:
With things we are a part, with God the whole.
Let us remain under the Godhead's Tree:
The world is like a dream; our heart is He.

TREASURES

Serenity: the eagle's flight may show
That world and suffering are far below.
Soul's liberty is like the open sky;
Blessèd the mind who like a bird can fly.

Then Certitude: in winter's cold and storm
My home is in my heart: deep, strong, and warm.
Because I made my heart a holy shrine,
My soul belongs to God, and God is mine.

Submission: for this earthly life is still
A trial; let us rest in Heaven's Will.

And Confidence: if we do what we should,
The door is open for the saving Good.

There must be Combat too: without this load
We would not find the liberating Road.

RADIATION

Substance is Truth, the accidents are naught;
The Heart must radiate, Shrī Lallā thought.
She left her home and dancèd in the street:
Naked her body's gold, and drunk her feet.

The inmost we don't always have to hide;
The inward and the outward coincide.
World veils and unveils, it is Māyā's mood —

It is the Godhead's Play; and Truth is nude.

SYNTHESIS

Truth, Way and Virtue: threefold is the Path
From Earth to Heaven. First discriminate
Between Reality and Dream; then pray:
Invoke the Name and reach the Godhead's Gate.

Then Virtue: for we must conform our selves
To That which we believe, adapt our soul
To That which saves. Our very breath should be
One with our Faith and with our highest Goal.

THE THREEFOLD PATH

Truth, Way and Virtue: Heaven gave us three
Tremendous Treasures, for each faculty:
Truth means to think; Remembrance means to do;
and Character — soul's Beauty — means to be.

WAR

No peace with weakness: with our selfish soul
And idle dreams; the worldly powers might
Seduce and poison us. We have no choice;
Our weapon is God's Name. We have to fight.

Truth gives no strength without humility.
Darkness means war; Light's war means victory.

PEACE

Our soul belongs to God, not to the loud
And harmful ringing of the restless mind.
Serenity is Beauty of the True;
It is in Beauty that our Peace we find.

If happiness you want, be calm and wise;
In God we rest. And Peace is Paradise.

PRESENCE

Forget that there is space and time: forget
The near and far, before and after; yet
Know that the Sovereign Good is always "Here"
And that in Heaven's "Now" there is no fear.

In this Eternal "Now" thy heart should live
And in this "Here", in its Infinity,
Thou hast thy home. Thy very breathing give
To Him Whose Presence shows us what to be.

CONTENTMENT

If you have reached a mountain's very top
Further you cannot go; you have to stop.
You wonder at the glory of the peak;
But we are heavy, and our acts are weak.

With counting flow'rs our time we cannot spend;
Our life must have a sense; dreams have an end.
Contentment is the station of the just;
His core is Truth and Bliss; the rest is dust.

Limitless is the Center; and if you
Are wise, your thought of God is always new.

BODY AND MIND

High in the mountains is the eagle's nest;
You think about the mountain's wondrous height
And then you feel the body's helpless weight.
What do you want? God's Presence is your rest.

Do not regret a height of any kind;
God is the Sky; the eagle is your mind.

ESSENTIALITY

What makes us happy? It is the Essential;
No happiness in dust and agitation!
Let the Essential be our Morning Star;
The sense of life is Truth and Liberation —

Truth with Felicity is what we are.

SILENCE

How can we find our rest in restless things,
In play and dreams to which desire clings?
If happiness you want, then close your eyes;
Silence is gold; and Peace is Paradise.

No heaviness is felt, no noise is heard;
Yet in this naught: God's Presence and His Word.

WILL AND WAY

God's Truth is constant like the Morning Star.
Our will is not as good as what we seek;
"Spirit is willing but the flesh is weak."
Ours is the evil, and the Good is far.

This does not mean that hopeless we should stay;
Where there's a will, there also is a way.
Trusting in God, always remember this:
Patience and Faith mean Everlasting Bliss.

And where we pray, there is the Godhead's Throne;
Who knows that God is near, is not alone.

FAITH AND PATIENCE

Do not complain; for Being's Melody
Flows from the strings of Everlasting Peace;
The breath of Māyā is Serenity.

And faith and patience are Salvation's Keys.
Love's price is heavy; light is Mercy's load.
Happy the soul who toward the Godhead flees —

A blessèd instant is the freeing Road.
Our life is hidden in a single call
From heart to God; the saving Word is all.

THE SUMMIT

What was the greatest moment of our life?
Where the most happiness, in which event?
Was it a day of glory, or of love?
A moment we with holy people spent?

It must have been the moment we met God.
He entered into time, we don't know how;
But time is always there, and God is near;
And so the summit of our life is Now.

THE CORE

I love because I love; this word is more
Than just a feeling, it is Wisdom's core.
Love God without conditions; the Most High
Will love thee too and will not ask thee why.

NOSTALGIA

Nostalgia does not mean disharmony;
The web of states is Beauty's alchemy.
Where is the peerless island of our tales?
The Truth we feel, yet our desire fails.

A saint ascended in a golden car
Of light; for others, Paradise is far.
For the true lover, Heaven's shore is near —
The song of Apsaras his heart may hear.

REMEMBRANCE

O Thou whose Name is sweetest remedy
And whose remembrance heals our soul's disease:
With Thee each moment is Eternity —
A drop from Heaven that consoles and frees.

THE ROAD

Say "yes" to God, God will say "yes" to thee;
To Heaven's gate this is the golden key.
About my earthly road I do not care;
It may be long; short is God's road to me.

CONTENTS

I. The Garland

II. Answers

III. Virgin Nature

IV. Creatures

V. Road to the Heart

BY THE SAME AUTHOR

The Transcendent Unity of Religions, *1953*
Revised Edition, *1975, 1984, The Theosophical Publishing House, 1993*

Spiritual Perspectives and Human Facts, *1954, 1969*
New Translation, *Perennial Books, 1987*

Gnosis: Divine Wisdom, *1959, 1978, Perennial Books 1990*

Stations of Wisdom, *1961, 1980*
New Translation, *World Wisdom Books, 1995*

Understanding Islam, *1963, 1965, 1972, 1976, 1979, 1981, 1986,
1989*
New Translation, *World Wisdom Books, 1994*

Light on the Ancient Worlds, *1966, World Wisdom Books, 1984*

In the Tracks of Buddhism, *1968, 1989*
New Translation, Treasures of Buddhism, *World Wisdom Books, 1993*

Logic and Transcendence, *1975, Perennial Books, 1984*

Esoterism as Principle and as Way, *Perennial Books, 1981, 1990*

Castes and Races, *Perennial Books, 1959, 1982*

Sufism: Veil and Quintessence, *World Wisdom Books, 1981*

From the Divine to the Human, *World Wisdom Books, 1982*

Christianity/Islam, *World Wisdom Books, 1985*

*The Essential Writings of Frithjof Schuon (S. H. Nasr, Ed.)
1986, Element, 1991*

Survey of Metaphysics & Esoterism, *World Wisdom Books, 1986*

In the Face of the Absolute, *World Wisdom Books, 1989, 1994*

The Feathered Sun: Plains Indians in Art & Philosophy,
World Wisdom Books, 1990

To Have a Center, *World Wisdom Books, 1990*

Roots of the Human Condition, *World Wisdom Books, 1991*

Images of Primordial & Mystic Beauty: Paintings by Frithjof Schuon,
Abodes, 1992

Echoes of Perennial Wisdom, *World Wisdom Books, 1992*

The Play of Masks, *World Wisdom Books, 1992*

The Transfiguration of Man, *World Wisdom Books, in preparation*